Reading SRA Mastery Plus

Teacher's Guide

Level 6

Siegfried Engelmann
Jean Osborn
Steve Osborn
Leslie Zoref

A Division of The McGraw·Hill Companies

Columbus, Ohio

Which *Reading Mastery* Program Is Right for Your Students?

The Level 6 *Reading Mastery* program is available in two versions: *Reading Mastery* Classic option and *Reading Mastery Plus* option. The Classic option is a reading-only program; the *Plus* option is a complete language-arts program that teaches both reading and language.

The core reading components (teacher materials, student textbooks, student workbook) of both versions are identical. The *Plus* option, however, features several additional language-arts components—a *Language Arts Guide,* a *Literature Anthology,* a *Literature Guide,* an *Activities across the Curriculum* project book, and a *Testing and Management Handbook.*

If your students need a complete language-arts program, select *Reading Mastery Plus,* Level 6. If your students need a reading-only program, select *Reading Mastery*, Classic option, Level 6. If you select the Classic option, you can always expand it later by adding one or more of the language-arts components from the *Plus* option, all of which are available for separate purchase.

www.sra4kids.com

SRA/McGraw-Hill

*A Division of The **McGraw·Hill** Companies*

Send all inquiries to:
SRA/McGraw-Hill
8787 Orion Place
Columbus, OH 43240-4027

Printed in the United States of America.

ISBN 0-07-569181-7

1 2 3 4 5 6 7 8 9 RRW 06 05 04 03 02 01

gift

Contents

Program Overview

Reading Mastery Plus, Level 6, is a revised and expanded version of *Reading Mastery 6,* the widely used direct instruction reading program that has proved effective in classrooms nationwide for more than two decades.

Like the previous edition of the program, *Reading Mastery Plus,* Level 6, features extensive practice in decoding, vocabulary building, comprehension strategies, and writing. To this solid core, the revised program adds several new components and activities, including a wide range of open-ended comprehension questions, an extensive literature anthology, and daily practice lessons in the language arts.

Reading Mastery Plus, Level 6, is for students who read at about a 6.0 grade level as measured by a standardized achievement test. The program can be used with students who have successfully completed *Reading Mastery Plus,* Level 5, or any other fifth-grade reading program. A placement test (see page 50) is provided to help you evaluate your students' reading level and determine appropriate placement in the *Reading Mastery Plus* series.

Key Features

Throughout its many components, *Reading Mastery Plus,* Level 6, consistently emphasizes nine key features of effective reading instruction. Following is a brief overview of these nine features.

Extensive and Varied Reading Selections

The student textbooks in *Reading Mastery Plus,* Level 6, contain a broad array of classic and contemporary selections for daily group reading. In the course of the program, students read four classic novels, as well as short stories, factual articles, biographies, myths, folktales, and poems. Novels and other longer selections are divided into chapters or parts and are presented over a span of lessons.

In addition, students read a literature anthology that contains a dozen stories of established literary value. Also included in the anthology are study outlines for several well-known children's novels.

Focused Comprehension Questions

The teacher materials for the textbook feature carefully sequenced literal and inferential comprehension questions that you ask before, during, and after reading. Students interact with you and with each other as they answer these questions, both orally and in writing. The questions focus on several important comprehension concepts, such as understanding perspectives, identifying motives, developing vocabulary, and interpreting themes.

Specific Comprehension Exercises

In addition to answering questions about their reading, students complete a variety of exercises that teach specific comprehension concepts and strategies. Particular emphasis is placed on identifying contradictions, interpreting figurative language, making inferences, and analyzing logic. Students also study maps, interpret graphs, and practice filling out forms.

Background Knowledge

Many of the textbook and *Literature Anthology* selections are preceded by short passages that provide important background information. Students use this information to comprehend the selections more fully. The program also contains longer factual articles that prepare students for reading and understanding the different types of expository prose found in social studies and science textbooks.

Reading Fluency

Rapid and accurate decoding (reading fluency) is a prerequisite for good comprehension. *Reading Mastery Plus* builds fluency by offering daily practice in oral and silent reading in a variety of contexts. Students begin each lesson by orally reading lists of words they will encounter in the reading selection for that lesson. Then individual students take turns reading the first part of the selection aloud. Afterward, the students read the rest of the selection silently. Finally, they receive further fluency practice by reading part of the selection aloud to a partner. Individual reading checkouts in the *Testing and Management*

Handbook allow you to monitor your students' progress in reading fluency.

Vocabulary Building

Direct and explicit vocabulary instruction is part of every lesson in *Reading Mastery Plus.* Before reading a selection, students discuss the meanings of important vocabulary words and phrases that will appear in the selection, and they practice using these words in various contexts. Then students encounter the vocabulary words as they read the selection. Finally, they complete written vocabulary exercises. Because repeated practice with new words is essential to vocabulary acquisition, these written exercises continually review all vocabulary words taught in the program.

Literary Analysis

Many of the comprehension activities in the program encourage students to analyze the literary aspects of their reading selections. For example, students compare the traits of different characters and project themselves into the stories. They also describe settings, compare plots, and discuss themes and morals. These activities build students' analytical skills and interpretive strategies.

Daily Writing

Students complete a writing assignment in every lesson of the program. Many of these assignments ask students to make judgments about the reading selections and to justify their judgments with specific evidence from the selection. Other assignments encourage students to interpret stories according to their own experiences or to relate story events to their own lives. In some lessons, students write stories and poems of their own.

Extension Activities

In addition to the core textbook, the workbook, and the literature anthology, the program offers a variety of extension activities. These activities improve students' language and writing skills, test-taking strategies, and ability to make cross-curricular connections.

Program Components

The core components of *Reading Mastery Plus,* Level 6, include the student textbooks, the student workbook, and the teacher presentation books. These components con-

tain 120 daily lessons with word-practice and vocabulary activities, oral and silent reading, comprehension questions, skill exercises, and writing assignments.

The *Literature Anthology* is an important component of the program. Students read a story from the anthology after every tenth textbook lesson. Although the students read the anthology stories independently, several comprehension and interpretation activities are provided for use with these stories. These activities appear at the beginning and end of each story. Directions for presenting the activities appear in the *Literature Guide.* The *Literature Anthology* also contains study outlines for four well-known novels that the students read independently.

Reading Mastery Plus, Level 6, also offers several extension components, including the *Language Arts Guide, Activities across the Curriculum,* and the *Testing and*

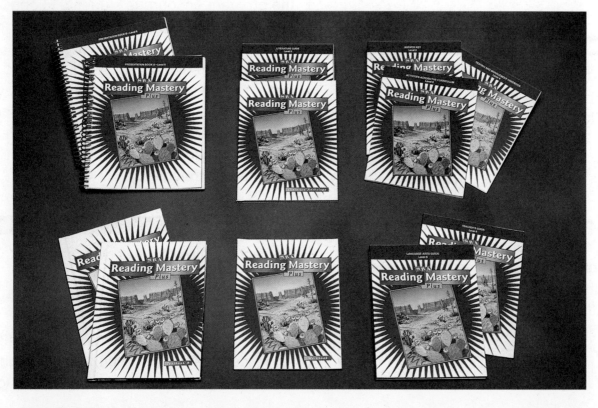

Management Handbook. This *Teacher's Guide* and the *Answer Key* are included as well.

The following sections explain each component in more detail.

Student Textbooks

These two nonconsumable hardbound books (A and B) contain a wide variety of reading selections. Each textbook is composed of two 30-lesson thematic units. The units for Textbook A are "Skilled Hands" (lessons 1–30) and "Finding Yourself" (lessons 31–60). The units for Textbook B are "American Adventures" (lessons 61–90) and "Tom Sawyer" (lessons 91–120).

Selections in the textbooks are preceded by word lists and vocabulary activities and followed by comprehension questions and a writing assignment. Many lessons include concept and strategy exercises and story background passages.

The textbook reading selections range from factual articles to full-length novels and brief poems. Here is a partial list by genre. (For a complete list, see the table of contents in each textbook.)

- Novels: *Tom Sawyer; Sara Crewe; The Odyssey; The Cruise of the Dazzler*

- Factual Articles: "Children at Work"; "Pirates on the Bay"; "Life in the 1840s"

- Contemporary short stories: "The Doughnuts"; "The Spider, the Cave, and the Pottery Bowl"; "Mrs. Dunn's Lovely, Lovely Farm"

- Folktales and myths: "The Table, the Donkey, and the Stick"; "Persephone"

- Poems: "Written in March"; "Casey at the Bat"; "Miracles"

- Biography: Harriet Tubman

- Play: *All in Favor*

Student Workbook

This consumable softbound book contains 120 two-sided worksheets perforated for easy removal. Students complete one worksheet during each daily lesson. After the worksheets have been graded, they can be removed from the workbook and taken home.

Most workbook exercises directly relate to the readings in the student textbooks. A typical workbook lesson contains questions about the textbook selection, vocabulary activities, and comprehension strategy exercises. Some lessons feature map interpretation, crossword puzzles, and other activities that approach the textbook content from a variety of learning perspectives.

Presentation Books

These two spiral-bound books (A and B) feature detailed direct-instruction scripts for presenting all 120 daily lessons in the program. *Presentation Book A* covers lessons 1–60; *Presentation Book B* covers lessons 61–120.

Each lesson in the presentation books is divided into a series of exercises that specify teacher instructions and student responses. For ease of use, the presentation books include reproductions of all the word lists and stories from the student textbooks.

Literature Anthology

This anthology, which is accompanied by a separate teacher's guide, contains classic and contemporary stories by Isaac Bashevis Singer, Mildred Taylor, Pam Conrad, and other well-known children's authors. (For a complete list, see the table of contents in the anthology.)

Students read the anthology stories independently. Each story is preceded by a background passage that enhances comprehension. The *Literature Guide* includes a range of comprehension activities, such as vocabulary exercises, story questions, and discussion and writing topics.

Language Arts Guide

This extensive guide features activities designed to integrate reading with the other language arts. The guide consists of blackline masters for the daily worksheets and accompanying teacher material. Topics include book parts, capitalization, comprehension skills, grammar, punctuation, reference sources, vocabulary, word parts, and writing skills. Students complete one language-arts worksheet after every textbook lesson. (For a complete list of activities, see the Index of Skills for the *Language Arts Guide* on page 54 of this Teacher's Guide.)

Activities across the Curriculum

This collection of activities connects *Reading Mastery Plus* to science, social studies, geography, music, art, and other content areas. The activities and accompanying blackline masters provide new contexts for using comprehension strategies, and they encourage the use of reference skills. (For a complete list of activities, see *Activities across the Curriculum.*)

Testing and Management Handbook

This handbook contains a complete set of mastery tests that you can use to measure student progress in the program. Tests occur after every tenth lesson, with a unit test appearing after every thirtieth lesson. The handbook also includes the Placement Test, remedial exercises, and suggestions for interpreting the test results.

Answer Key

This booklet lists the answers to all the workbook and textbook activities. Workbook pages are reproduced with answers in place. Answers for textbook exercises are listed separately. Guidelines for evaluating writing assignments are included as well.

Teacher's Guide

The *Teacher's Guide* (which you are now reading) contains specific advice to help you implement *Reading Mastery Plus*, Level 6, in your classroom. The guide includes an overview of the program, a complete sample lesson, and classroom-tested suggestions for teaching every part of the program. It also includes the Placement Test, scope-and-sequence charts, behavioral objectives, a Skills Profile Folder, and sample lessons from each component of the program.

Sample Lesson

The textbooks and the workbook in *Reading Mastery Plus,* Level 6, contain 120 daily lessons. Instructions for presenting these lessons appear in the presentation books. The *Literature Anthology,* which is used after every tenth textbook lesson, has its own guide.

The following sample lesson (lesson 57) appears in *Presentation Book A.* Like every other lesson in the program, lesson 57 is divided into three parts: Before Reading, Reading, and After Reading. In the Before Reading segment, students prepare to read the textbook selection by studying lists of words, completing vocabulary exercises, and developing comprehension strategies. In the Reading segment, students read the textbook selection orally and silently and answer oral comprehension questions. Finally, in the After Reading segment, students complete vocabulary, comprehension, and writing activities in the workbook and textbook. They also work on extension activities.

The presentation books contain all the teacher directions and student materials needed to present the main part of the lessons. The teacher directions consist of carefully worded exercises that teach specific skills and strategies. The following typographic conventions are used:

- Words you say appear in blue type.

- Words you emphasize appear in **bold blue type.**

- Instructions for you to follow appear in black roman type and are enclosed in parentheses.

- Student responses appear in *black italic type.*

- Reproductions of student material, such as word lists and the textbook selections, appear in boxes. These boxes are inserted into the teacher directions for ease of reference.

Before Reading

Students begin almost every lesson by orally reading lists of words in their textbooks. In the first exercise of lesson 57, you read hard words that will appear in the textbook selection. Then students read the words.

BEFORE READING

Have students find lesson 57, part A, in their textbooks.

EXERCISE 1

HARD WORDS

1. Look at column 1.
- These are hard words from your textbook stories.

1. **heron**	4. **wilderness**
2. **trio**	5. **gallant**
3. **Sylvia**	6. **pigeon**

2. Word 1 is **heron**. Everybody, what word? (Signal.) *Heron.*
   • (Repeat this procedure for every word in the column.)
3. Let's read the words again.
4. Word 1. Everybody, what word? (Signal.) *Heron.*
   • (Repeat this procedure for every word in the column.)
5. (Repeat the column until firm.)

In exercise 2, students practice reading words on their own, without your model.

EXERCISE 2

WORD PRACTICE

1. Look at column 2.
   • We're going to practice these words.

---

1. Circe	3. Scylla
2. Calypso	

---

2. Word 1. Everybody, what word? (Signal.) *Circe.*
   • (Repeat this procedure for every word in the column.)
3. (Repeat the column until firm.)

In exercise 3, students read new vocabulary words prior to learning their definitions.

EXERCISE 3

NEW VOCABULARY

1. Look at column 3.
   • First we'll read the words in this column. Then we'll read their definitions.

---

1. heron	5. gallant
2. foster parent	6. trio
3. huckleberry	7. game
4. bough	

---

2. Word 1. Everybody, what word? (Signal.) *Heron.*
   • (Repeat this procedure for every word in the column.)
3. (Repeat the column until firm.)

In exercise 4, students read definitions of the vocabulary words that will appear in the reading selections. After reading the definitions, they answer questions about the words or practice using them in context.

EXERCISE 4

VOCABULARY DEFINITIONS

1. Everybody, find part B. ✓
   • These are definitions for the words you just read.
2. (For each word, call on a student to read the definition and the item. Then ask the student to complete the item.)

1. **heron**—*Herons* are birds that wade through water and eat frogs and fish. Herons usually have tall, thin legs and a long, S-shaped neck. The picture shows a *white heron.*
   • Describe a heron.

   • What's the answer? (Ideas: *It has tall, thin legs and a long, S-shaped neck; it wades through water and eats frogs and fish.*)

2. **foster parent**—A *foster parent* is somebody who brings up a child but is not the child's real parent.
   • What do we call somebody who brings up a child but is not the child's real parent?

   • What's the answer? (Response: *A foster parent.*)

3. **huckleberry**—A *huckleberry* is a small purple or black berry that grows on bushes.
   • What is a huckleberry?

   • What's the answer? (Idea: *A small purple or black berry that grows on bushes.*)

4. **bough**—A *bough* of a tree is a branch of the tree.
   • What is a branch of a tree?

   • What's the answer? (Response: *A bough.*)

5. **gallant**—Somebody who is *gallant* is brave and noble.
   • What's another way of saying *He was a noble warrior*?

   • What's the answer? (Response: *He was a gallant warrior.*)

6. **trio**—A *trio* is a group of three.
   • What's another way of saying *A group of three went to the river*?

   • What's the answer? (Response: *A trio went to the river.*)

7. **game**—Wild animals that are hunted are called *game.*
   • What do we call wild animals that are hunted?

   • What's the answer? (Response: *Game.*)

The Before Reading segment concludes with exercise 5, in which students learn about using inference as a comprehension strategy. Students read an inference exercise orally and discuss the answers.

INFERENCE

1. Everybody, turn to part D at the end of today's story. ✓
   • (Call on individual students to read several sentences each.)
   • (At the end of each section, present the questions for that section.)

Write the answers for items 1–8.
   You have to answer different types of questions about the passages you read. Some questions are answered by words in the passage. Other questions are *not* answered by words in the passage. You have to figure out the answer by making a deduction.

   • What do you use to answer the first kind of question? (Idea: *Words in the passage.*)
   • What do you use to answer the second kind of question? (Idea: *A deduction.*)

   The following passage includes both types of questions.
More about Ecology
   Two hundred years ago, many people were not concerned with ecology. They believed there was no end to the different types of wildlife, so they killed wild animals by the hundreds of thousands. When we look back on these killings, we may feel shocked. But for the people who lived two hundred years ago, wild animals seemed to be as plentiful as weeds.
   Because of these killings, more than a hundred types of animals have become extinct since 1800. An animal is extinct when there are no more animals of that type.
   One type of extinct animal is the passenger pigeon. At one time, these birds were so plentiful that flocks of them used to blacken the sky. Now the passenger pigeon is gone forever. Think of that. You will never get to see a living passenger

pigeon or any of the other animals that have become extinct. The only place you can see those animals is in a museum, where they are stuffed and mounted.

1. Are house cats extinct?

- What's the answer? (Response: *No.*)

2. Is that question answered by **words** or a **deduction**?

- What's the answer? (Response: *Deduction.*)
- That's right, the passage does not contain this sentence: "House cats are not extinct." You figure out the answer by making a deduction.
- Here's the deduction: **Animals are extinct when there are no more animals of that type. There are still many house cats. Therefore, house cats are not extinct.**

3. Name one type of extinct animal.

- What's the answer? (Response: *The passenger pigeon.*)

4. **Words** or **deduction**?

- Is the question answered by **words** or by a **deduction**? (Response: *Words.*)
- Read the sentence that contains words that answer the question. (Response: *One type of extinct animal is the passenger pigeon.*)

5. How many types of animals have become extinct since 1800?

- What's the answer? (Response: *More than a hundred.*)

6. **Words** or **deduction**?

- Is the question answered by **words** or by a **deduction**? (Response: *Words.*)

- Read the sentence that contains the words that answer the question. (Response: *Because of these killings, more than a hundred types of animals have become extinct since 1800.*)

7. The dodo bird is extinct. How many animals of that type are alive today?

- What's the answer? (Idea: *None.*)

8. **Words** or **deduction**?

- Is the question answered by **words** or by a **deduction**? (Response: *Deduction.*)
- Here's the deduction: **Animals are extinct when there are no more animals of that type. The dodo bird is extinct. Therefore, there are no more animals of that type.**
- You'll write the answers later.

Reading

> In the Reading segment of the lesson, students read the textbook selection and answer comprehension questions. Most textbook selections begin with a focus question. This question highlights a key element of the textbook selection. Students will answer the focus question after they finish reading the selection.

READING

FOCUS QUESTION

1. Everybody, find part C. ✓
2. What's the focus question for today's lesson? (Response: *How did Sylvia feel about living on her foster mother's farm?*)

Students usually read the first part of the textbook selection aloud. This activity builds decoding fluency and improves comprehension. Proficient readers sometimes have the option of reading the first part silently.

EXERCISE 7

READING ALOUD (OPTIONAL)

1. We're going to read aloud to the diamond.
   - (Call on individual students to read several sentences each.)

A White Heron
by Sarah Orne Jewett
Part 1
Focus Question: How did Sylvia feel about living on her foster mother's farm?

The woods were filled with shadows one June evening, but a bright sunset still glimmered faintly among the trunks of the trees. A girl named Sylvia was driving a cow from the pasture to her home. Sylvia had spent more than an hour looking for the cow and had finally found her hiding behind a huckleberry bush.

Sylvia and the cow were going away from the sunset and into the dark woods. But they were familiar with the path, and the darkness did not bother them.

Sylvia wondered what her foster mother, Mrs. Tilley, would say because they were so late. But Mrs. Tilley knew how difficult it was to find the cow. She had chased the beast many times herself. As she waited, she was only thankful that Sylvia could help her. Sylvia seemed to love the out-of-doors, and Mrs. Tilley thought that being outdoors was a good change for an orphan girl who had grown up in a town.

The companions followed the shady road. The cow took slow steps, and the girl took very fast ones. The cow stopped at the brook to drink, and Sylvia stood still and waited. She let her bare feet cool themselves in the water while the great twilight moths struck softly against her. She waded on through the brook as the cow moved away, and she listened to the waterbirds with pleasure.

There was a stirring in the great boughs overhead. They were full of little birds that seemed to be wide awake and going about their business. Sylvia began to feel sleepy as she walked along. However, it was not much farther to the house, and the air was soft and sweet.

She was not often in the woods so late as this. The darkness made her feel as if she were a part of the gray shadows and the moving leaves. She was thinking how long it seemed since she had first come to her foster mother's farm a year ago. Sylvia wondered if everything was still going on in the noisy town just the same as when she had lived there. ♦

In exercise 8, students read the rest of the selection silently. After they finish, you ask a series of comprehension questions, including a restatement of the Focus Question. These after-reading questions primarily involve literary interpretation and comprehension strategies.

EXERCISE 8

SILENT READING

1. Read the rest of the lesson to yourselves and be ready to answer some questions.

It seemed to Sylvia that she had never been alive at all before she came to live at her foster mother's farm. It was a beautiful place to live, and she never wished to go back to the town. The thought of the children who used to chase and frighten her made her hurry along the path to escape from the shadows of the trees.

Suddenly, she was horror-struck to hear a clear whistle not very far away. It was not a bird's whistle. It sounded more like a boy's. Sylvia stepped aside into the bushes, but she was too late. The whistler had discovered her, and he called out in a cheerful voice, "Hello, little girl, how far is it to the road?"

Trembling, Sylvia answered quietly, "A long distance."

She did not dare to look at the tall young man, who carried a gun over his shoulder. But Sylvia came out of the bushes and again followed the cow, while the young man walked alongside her.

"I have been hunting for some birds," the stranger said kindly, "and I have lost my way. Don't be afraid," he added gallantly. "Speak up and tell me what your name is and whether you think I can spend the night at your house and go out hunting early in the morning." ★

Sylvia was more alarmed than before. Would her foster mother blame her for this? She hung her head, but she managed to answer "Sylvia" when her companion again asked her name.

Mrs. Tilley was standing in the doorway when the trio came into view. The cow gave a loud moo as if to explain the situation.

Mrs. Tilley said, "Yes, you'd better speak up for yourself, you naughty old cow! Where'd she hide herself this time, Sylvia?" But Sylvia kept silent.

The young man stood his gun beside the door and dropped a heavy gamebag next to it. Then he said good evening to Mrs. Tilley. He repeated his story and asked if he could have a night's lodging.

"Put me anywhere you like," he said. "I must be off early in the morning, before day, but I am very hungry indeed. Could you give me some milk?"

"Dear sakes, yes," said Mrs. Tilley. "You might do better if you went out to the main road, but you're welcome to what we've got. I'll milk the cow right now, and you

make yourself at home. Now step round and set a plate for the gentleman, Sylvia!"

Sylvia promptly stepped. She was glad to have something to do, and she was hungry herself.

- How did Sylvia feel about living on her foster mother's farm? (Ideas: *She loved being outdoors; the farm made her feel alive.*)
- Why didn't Sylvia like the town? (Ideas: *The other children made fun of her; it was noisy and crowded.*)
- Why do you think Sylvia didn't dare to look at the young man? (Ideas: *She was afraid of him; he was a stranger; she was shy.*)
- How do you think Sylvia feels about hunting? Explain your answer. (Ideas: *She probably doesn't like hunting because she loves living things; she probably doesn't like hunting because guns are noisy.*)
- What do you think will happen in the next part of the story? (Ideas: *The stranger will ask Sylvia to go hunting with him; the stranger will rob Sylvia and her foster mother.*)

The Reading segment concludes with an optional activity, Paired Practice. For this exercise, pairs of students read to each other as you observe and assist them.

EXERCISE 9

PAIRED PRACTICE (OPTIONAL)

1. Now you'll read in pairs.
- Whoever read second the last time will read first today.
- Remember to start at the diamond and switch at the star.
2. (Observe students and answer questions as needed.)

After Reading

Students begin the After Reading segment by working independently in their workbooks and textbooks.

AFTER READING

EXERCISE 10

INDEPENDENT WORK

1. Do all the items in your workbook and textbook for this lesson.
2. (The independent work in this lesson includes the following activities.)
   - Story details
   - Vocabulary
   - Figurative language
   - Deductions
   - Character traits
   - Comparisons
   - Inference
   - Vocabulary review
   - Comprehension
   - Writing

Students first complete the workbook activities, which contain comprehension and vocabulary exercises. Many of these exercises directly relate to the reading selection. Students write their answers in the workbook itself.

In part A of the workbook for lesson 57, students answer literal questions about the day's reading selection. These questions highlight important events and concepts in the story.

A STORY DETAILS

Write or circle the answers.

1. Sylvia was __ who lived on a farm.
   - a vacationer • a farmhand • an orphan

2. Where had Sylvia lived before coming to the farm?

   _____

3. Sylvia thought she had never been __ at all before coming to the farm.
   - scared • alive • punished

4. Which place did Sylvia enjoy more, the town or the farm?

   _____

5. How had the children in town treated Sylvia?

   _____

6. What was the young man doing in the woods?

   _____

7. Was Sylvia bold or shy?

   _____

8. What was the name of the person who owned the farm?

   _____

9. That person was Sylvia's __.
   - employer • mother • foster parent

In part B, students use vocabulary words in context. They have already studied these words and have read them in the textbook selections.

B VOCABULARY

Write the correct words in the blanks.

regarded	suitable
appealed	humiliating
unprecedented	maneuvered

1. The starving boy _____ to the sympathy of the crowd.

2. They _____ the criminal as a dangerous person.

3. He _____ the shopping cart past the fallen cans.

In part C, students review previously learned types of figurative language, including similes, metaphors, and exaggeration.

C FIGURATIVE LANGUAGE

For each statement, write **simile, metaphor,** or **exaggeration.**

1. Her face was like a pale star.

_____

2. The apartment was a prison.

_____

3. The day was like a dream.

_____

In part D, students practice completing deductions, another previously learned comprehension strategy.

D DEDUCTIONS

Complete each deduction.

Every element has an atomic weight. Argon is an element.

1. What's the conclusion about argon?

_____

Horses eat grass. A palomino is a horse.

2. What's the conclusion about a palomino?

_____

In part E, students sharpen their literary skills by identifying character traits. Other literary exercises focus on character motives, perspectives, settings, plots, and themes.

E CHARACTER TRAITS

Write whether each phrase describes **Sylvia, Mrs. Tilley,** or **the stranger.**

1. Very shy

_____

2. Whistled loudly

_____

3. An orphan

_____

> The last workbook exercise is part F, where students review their textbook stories by making comparisons.

F COMPARISONS

Write **Odyssey** if the event occurred in *The Odyssey*. Write **Yarn** if the event occurred in "Mystery Yarn."

1. Telemachus was one of the suitors.

   _____

2. Telemachus helped defeat the suitors.

   _____

3. The suitors took a test that involved unwinding string.

   _____

4. The suitors took a test that involved a bow and arrow.

   _____

After completing the workbook exercises, students complete independent activities in the textbook. These activities generally require longer answers than the workbook questions. Students write their answers on a separate piece of paper.

In this sample lesson, students have already completed parts A–C of the textbook in the Before Reading and Reading segments of the lesson. They begin their independent work with part D (Inference), which they previewed earlier in the lesson (see page 11).

D INFERENCE

Write the answers for items 1–8.

You have to answer different types of questions about the passages you read. Some questions are answered by words in the passage. Other questions are *not* answered by words in the passage. You have to figure out the answer by making a deduction.

The following passage includes both types of questions.

More about Ecology

Two hundred years ago, many people were not concerned with ecology. They believed there was no end to the different types of wildlife, so they killed wild animals by the hundreds of thousands. When we look back on these killings, we may feel shocked. But for the people who lived two hundred years ago, wild animals seemed to be as plentiful as weeds.

Because of these killings, more than a hundred types of animals have become extinct since 1800. An animal is extinct when there are no more animals of that type.

One type of extinct animal is the passenger pigeon. At one time, these birds were so plentiful that flocks of them used to blacken the sky. Now the passenger pigeon is gone forever. Think of that. You will never get to see a living passenger pigeon or any of the other animals that have become extinct. The only place you can see those animals is in a museum, where they are stuffed and mounted.

1. Are house cats extinct?
2. Is that question answered by **words** or a **deduction**?
3. Name one type of extinct animal.
4. **Words** or **deduction**?
5. How many types of animals have become extinct since 1800?
6. **Words** or **deduction**?
7. The dodo bird is extinct. How many animals of that type are alive today?
8. **Words** or **deduction**?

In parts E and F, students receive additional practice with Deduction and Vocabulary exercises.

E DEDUCTIONS

Write the answers about the deductions.

Oliver believed that if he studied, he would pass the test. Oliver studied for the test.

1. So, what did Oliver believe would happen?

Nadia believed that if you ate an apple a day you would stay healthy. Nadia ate an apple every day.

2. So, what did Nadia believe would happen?

F VOCABULARY REVIEW

unprecedented
maneuver
devoted
spurn
endured
regard

For each item, write the correct word.

1. When you move skillfully, you ______.
2. When you consider something, you ______ it.
3. Something that has never occurred before is ______.

In part G of the textbook, students write the answers to interpretive comprehension questions about the reading selection. In many cases, these questions are the same as those presented earlier by the teacher, so students have already thought about their answers.

G COMPREHENSION

Write the answers.
1. How did Sylvia feel about living on her foster mother's farm?
2. Why didn't Sylvia like the town?
3. Why do you think Sylvia didn't dare to look at the young man?
4. How do you think Sylvia feels about hunting? Explain your answer.

The final textbook exercise is the writing assignment. These assignments take many forms. In some, students express their opinions about the textbook selections or pretend to be story characters. In others, they use the selection as a springboard for their own imaginative responses.

H WRITING

Where would you rather live, on a farm or in a town?
 Write an essay that explains your answer. Try to answer the following questions:
 • What are the advantages of living on a farm?
 • What are the disadvantages of living on a farm?
 • What are the advantages of living in a town?
 • What are the disadvantages of living in a town?

After students complete the workbook and textbook activities, you conduct a workcheck.

EXERCISE 11

WORKCHECK
1. (Using the Answer Key, read the questions and answers for the workbook.)
2. (Have students read their answers for the textbook activities.)
3. (Have two or three students read their writing assignments aloud. Comment on each assignment.)
4. (Have students correct and turn in their work.)

57

Lesson 57

Name _____

- **Past-tense** verbs express actions that have already happened.
- Past-tense verbs are usually formed by adding **d** or **ed** to the base verb.
- The form of past-tense verbs is the same for both singular and plural subjects.

A. Write the past-tense form of the verb to finish the sentence.

1. **mow**   Jamael _____ yards all last summer.

2. **wait**   Betsy _____ twenty minutes for Howard.

3. **explore**   The tourists _____ the mission ruins.

4. **watch**   I _____ in horror as the wall tumbled.

5. **help**   Kyle _____ his grandmother clean her attic.

B. For each item, circle the verb. Write present or past to show its tense.

                                                          Tense

1. Gordon erased the first paragraph of his essay.   _____

2. Do you object to the plan?   _____

3. Jeanne boasted about her new computer.   _____

4. Leslie talks too much!   _____

5. Suzi smiles easily.   _____

Presenting the Program

Reading Mastery Plus, Level 6, is a complete instructional program that you can present to an entire class or to smaller groups. This section of the *Teacher's Guide* gives general recommendations for presenting the program effectively. Detailed instructions for teaching specific exercises appear in the next section of the guide.

Scheduling the Reading Period

Every textbook lesson in *Reading Mastery Plus,* Level 6, consists of Before Reading, Reading, and After Reading segments. If possible, try to present all three segments consecutively. The workcheck and the extension activities, however, can be presented at any time after the students have completed the rest of the lesson.

The Before Reading segment—during which you present word practice, vocabulary, and comprehension exercises—usually takes about 15 minutes. The Reading segment—during which students read the textbook selection independently—lasts 30 to 45 minutes. The first part of the After Reading segment—during which students complete their workbook and textbook activities—takes about 30 minutes.

The time required for the workcheck and the extension activities varies, depending on the number of activities and the length of the workcheck. In general, at least 30 minutes is required. The workcheck can be presented immediately after students complete their independent work, later in the day, or just before the next day's lesson.

Here is one possible schedule for teaching a daily lesson:

- 8:45—9:00 Before Reading segment
- 9:00—9:45 Reading segment
- 9:45—10:15 After Reading segment
- 10:15—10:45 Workcheck and extension activities

If you divide your class into two groups for reading instruction, you can work with one group while the other group is completing the After Reading activities.

A story from the *Literature Anthology* can be scheduled after every ten textbook lessons. Students read the anthology stories independently, so the schedule for these days is more flexible.

Using the Presentation Books

The presentation books contain complete directions for presenting every textbook lesson in the program. The directions are carefully written to make the teaching clear and unambiguous. The program will be most effective if the directions are followed closely.

The presentation books use several typefaces and other scripting conventions:

- Words you say appear in blue type.

- Words you emphasize appear in **bold blue type.**

- Instructions for you to follow appear in black roman type and are enclosed in parentheses.

- Student responses appear in *black italic type.*

- Questions that require a group response begin with the word *Everybody* and are followed by a signal and the exact group response. For example: Everybody, what word? (Signal.) *Freight.*

- Questions for individual students do not include the word *Everybody* and do not require a signal. Possible responses for these questions are enclosed in parentheses, as follows:

  - For questions with exact answers, the student's response is preceded by the word *Response.* For example: Which is greater, the supply of Uncle Ulysses' doughnuts or the demand for doughnuts? (Response: *The supply.*)

  - For questions with variable answers, the student's response is enclosed in parentheses and preceded by the word *Idea.* For these questions, accept any answers that express the correct idea, no matter what the phrasing. For example: How did Mr. Gabby think they could increase the demand for doughnuts? (Idea: *By advertising the doughnuts.*)

Pacing the Lesson

You should present the daily lessons at a lively pace. Fast pacing keeps students thinking, encourages achievement, and reduces discipline problems.

With fast pacing, students are actively participating and are unlikely to get distracted. You can also cover more of the lesson and give students more practice in specific concepts and strategies.

To set a fast pace, present the exercises quickly, but don't rush students into making mistakes. Experience will help you determine the appropriate pace for your students. If you study each lesson before presenting it to students, you will be able to set a faster pace because you will not have to refer to the presentation book for every word.

Using Signals

All word-practice tasks and most vocabulary tasks require unison group responses. When students respond in unison, you know that every student is initiating a response and every student is practicing the task. You can also monitor every student's response and correct mistakes immediately.

The signal eliminates the problem of one student leading the rest of the group. You initiate unison responses by using an audible signal. Use the following procedure.

1. Ask the specified question.

2. Pause for about one second.

3. Make an audible signal, such as a clap, a tap, or a finger snap. An audible signal is necessary because students are looking at their textbooks, not at you.

4. Listen to the group response and correct any errors.

5. Move quickly to the next question.

The pause separates the question from the signal and ensures that every student hears the signal. The pause should always last about one second. When the pause is of a consistent and predictable length, the group will learn to respond on signal more readily.

Teaching to Mastery

All the exercises in the program should be taught to mastery. When an exercise is taught to mastery, every student in the group is able to respond to the questions and directions without making any mistakes.

Concepts and strategies taught in one lesson of the program are constantly applied and developed in subsequent lessons. When you teach a concept to mastery, students not only retain and apply the concept but are also prepared to learn related and more advanced concepts. By teaching every concept to mastery, you will help each student succeed.

Teaching Suggestions

This section of the *Teacher's Guide* presents specific teaching suggestions for each type of activity found in *Reading Mastery Plus,* Level 6. The activities are discussed in the order in which they appear in a lesson. Most discussions include a description and rationale for the activity, followed by specific teaching suggestions.

Word Practice

The word-practice exercises present words from the textbook selections. These words are organized into lists. Students practice reading the lists so they can read the words accurately in the textbook selections. You direct students to read the words aloud and in unison.

There are three main types of word lists:

- **Hard Words.** These words are difficult to decode. You read each word aloud, and then the group reads the word.

- **Word Practice.** These words are easy to decode. You ask, "Everybody, what word?" and the group reads the word.

- **New Vocabulary.** These words are defined later in the lesson. For now, you ask, "Everybody, what word?" and the group reads the word.

All three types of word lists appear in the sample lesson on pages 9 and 10 of this guide. One other type of list, Character

Names, appears in selected lessons. For this type, you read each name aloud, and then the group reads the name.

Teaching Suggestions

Here are some suggestions for effectively presenting word-practice exercises.

Maintain clear signals. For many exercises, you

1. Direct students to look at a word.

2. Say, "Everybody, what word?"

3. Pause.

4. Signal.

Students respond in unison. Use a clap or some other audible signal to indicate when students are to respond. Your signal should follow "Everybody, what word?" by about one second. The timing should always be the same—very rhythmical and predictable.

Position yourself so you can observe what students are doing. Do not just stand in front of the group as you present the word-practice exercises. Instead, walk among students and look at their mouths to make sure they're reading the words.

Focus on students who are most likely to make mistakes. Stand near one of these students as you present two or three words. Then move to another student. Observe whether students are

- looking at the appropriate words

- saying the words correctly

- responding on signal or merely waiting for others to lead them

Correct signal violations and slow responses. Some students may wait for other students to say the words. Unless all students respond together, you won't know which students are having trouble, and you won't be able to correct their mistakes.

To correct students who respond too soon or too late, say, "You have to wait for the signal" or "You are late." Then repeat the exercise, praising students who respond on signal. Make sure your signal is clear.

Correct monotone responses. Some students may respond in a monotone. These responses may indicate students do not know the words they are reading or are merely copying the responses of other students.

To correct slow or monotone responses, say, "That doesn't sound right. Listen to me." Then read the word in a normal speaking voice. Finally, have students read the word. Ask them to "Read it the way you talk."

Repeat each word that is read correctly by the group. For example, immediately after students read the word *advertise*, say, "Yes, *advertise*." Sometimes students read words incorrectly, and you don't hear their mistakes. If you routinely say each word after students read it, you give them a clear example of a correct reading.

Correct all word-reading errors immediately. Even if only one student in the group makes an error, correct the response as soon as you hear the error.

Use the following procedure.

1. Say the word.

2. Have students repeat the word.

3. Have students spell the word.

4. Have students read the word again.

5. Direct students to return to the first word in the column and read all the words in the column again.

The last step is important. Students soon learn that they must remember how to read all the words in a column.

Treat each column as the unit of mastery. The objective is for students to read all the words in each column quickly and without error. The unit of mastery is the column of words, not the individual word. Students must read all the words in one column correctly before you present the next column. When students master a column of words, they will probably be able to read those words correctly in the textbook selections.

Use individual turns. If you are unsure of some of your students' responses, give them individual turns reading the words in a column.

Establish a goal for good performance. If students continue to make errors after you have corrected them, give them a goal—a reason for trying to perform well. You can use the present performance of the group to promote improvement. For example, if students usually need four repetitions of a list before they can read it without error, challenge them to master the list with only three repetitions.

Work on your presentation. If students continue to make mistakes when reading columns of words, there may be problems with your presentation. Make sure you

- correct all errors immediately
- do not permit individual students to lead the group
- do not permit monotone responses
- use good pacing

If students are still having problems after you have worked on your presentation, try giving them more frequent individual turns. Some students may also be in the wrong level of the program. If necessary, readminister the placement test.

Vocabulary

Reading Mastery Plus, Level 6, teaches the meanings of about 500 vocabulary words and phrases. All new vocabulary words appear in teacher-directed exercises before they appear in a reading selection. The words are then reviewed in textbook and workbook exercises. The repeated appearance of vocabulary words ensures that students not only learn the words, but also use them in multiple contexts.

Three main types of exercises are used to teach and review vocabulary words:

- **Vocabulary Definitions.** Students read vocabulary definitions aloud and then answer questions about the words.
- **Vocabulary Review.** Students use vocabulary words to complete sentences that define the words.
- **Vocabulary in Context.** Students use context clues to determine correct usage of vocabulary words.

Vocabulary words are also reviewed in crossword puzzles and in various reading comprehension activities.

Vocabulary Definitions

These teacher-directed exercises appear in the Before Reading segment of almost every lesson in the program. The following example is typical:

B VOCABULARY DEFINITIONS

1. **revenge**—When you take *revenge* on someone, you get even with that person. Here's another way of saying *He got even with the robber: He took revenge on the robber.*
   - What's another way of saying *She got even with her sister*?
2. **unearthly**—When something is *unearthly,* it is unlike things you normally find on earth.
   - What would you call a rock that is unlike rocks you normally find on earth?
3. **neglect**—When you *neglect* something, you fail to take care of it.
   - What's another way of saying *She failed to take care of her dog*?
4. **custom**—A *custom* is a way of behaving that everybody follows.
   - What do we call a way of behaving that everybody follows?

The teacher asks an individual student to read a definition and answer the accompanying question. All words are defined in complete sentences composed of understandable words.

The definitions and accompanying questions take various forms. In item 1 above, for example, students read a definition of *revenge* that includes a sample sentence. They then repeat the sample sentence. In item 2, students read a definition of *unearthly* and then use the word to answer a question. In item 3, students read a definition of *neglect* and then say a sentence that contains the word.

The form of definition depends on the difficulty of the word and the word's typical use. Each definition is tailored to ensure maximum comprehension.

Vocabulary Review

After words are introduced in the Vocabulary Definitions exercise, they are systematically reviewed. For example, the words defined in lesson 11 appear in the Vocabulary Review exercise for lesson 12 and then in other vocabulary exercises. Here is the lesson 12 review exercise:

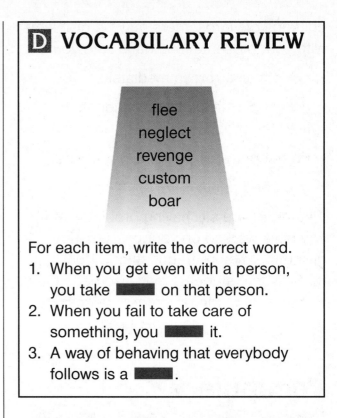

D VOCABULARY REVIEW

flee
neglect
revenge
custom
boar

For each item, write the correct word.
1. When you get even with a person, you take ▬▬ on that person.
2. When you fail to take care of something, you ▬▬ it.
3. A way of behaving that everybody follows is a ▬▬ .

Students do this exercise independently. First they read the words, all of which have been defined in previous lessons. Then they complete the accompanying definitions by selecting the correct words.

Vocabulary in Context

For the last type of vocabulary exercise, students use context clues to determine correct use of vocabulary words. Here is the context exercise for lesson 13, which appears in the workbook:

B VOCABULARY

Write the correct words in the blanks.

flasks	perils
neglected	minstrel
lice	custom
revenge	hideous
deeds	perish

1. The king was well known for his kind

   _____.

2. Inside the refrigerator were _____ of cool water.

3. Scylla was one of the most _____ creatures Odysseus saw.

4. After the feast, a _____ sang at the celebration.

5. These plants will _____ if it doesn't rain soon.

6. On his way home, Odysseus faced many

   _____.

7. Their hair was dirty and full of

   _____.

8. It was a _____ for the firstborn son to become king.

9. The children decided to take

   _____ on the bully.

Students first read the words, all of which have been previously defined and reviewed. Then they use context clues to select the correct words to complete the sentences.

Because this exercise appears in the workbook, students write the words directly in the sentences, further reinforcing correct use.

Teaching Suggestions

Here are some suggestions for teaching the vocabulary exercises effectively.

Make sure individual responses are heard by the group. For all questions about new vocabulary, only one student gives the answer. You may have to repeat that student's answer to make sure the entire group hears it.

Provide extra review for troublesome words. Take note of the vocabulary words that are still troublesome for students after two exercises. Review these words in subsequent lessons and at other times during the school day.

Accept all correct student responses. Sometimes students give a correct word meaning that is different from the meaning given in the vocabulary exercise. Accept all correct definitions and comment that some words have several meanings.

Correct all errors immediately. Most errors on vocabulary exercises occur when students must replace an entire phrase with a single word, or vice versa. For example, students learn that *encounter* means "come into contact with." They are then asked, "What's another way of saying *He came into contact with misfortune*?" Some students may answer, "He encountered contact with misfortune."

Correct errors of this type by emphasizing the correct answer and then repeating the task. For example:

1. The answer is **He encountered misfortune.**

- *Say that sentence.* (Response: *He encountered misfortune.*)

2. What's another way of saying **He came into contact with misfortune**? (Response: *He encountered misfortune.*)

Use a similar procedure to correct errors on other vocabulary tasks. First emphasize the correct answer and then repeat the question. For students who still have trouble, try modeling the answer by "thinking aloud" before you signal.

Comprehension Concepts

In *Reading Mastery Plus,* Level 6, comprehension strategies are taught both in specific exercises and through comprehension questions. This section of the *Teacher's Guide* discusses the specific exercises. For a discussion of the comprehension questions, see page 43.

New comprehension exercises are typically presented by you in one or two consecutive lessons. In most cases, students then complete the exercises independently for at least three more consecutive lessons. Thereafter, the exercises are intermittently reviewed throughout the program.

The main comprehension strands in *Reading Mastery Plus,* Level 6, are listed in the next column. The numbers indicate only the consecutive lessons in which a particular concept is taught and practiced. For example, outlining is taught and prac-

ticed in *every* lesson from 15 to 28. Thereafter, it is intermittently reviewed.

- Main idea and outlining: 15–28
- Relevant information: 21–30
- Contradictions: 32–42
- Figurative language (similes, metaphors, exaggeration, sarcasm): 39–62
- Deductions and inferences: 54–64
- Referents and missing words: 66–75
- Combined sentences: 74–83
- Following directions: 81–84
- Reference books: 85–90
- Maps and graphs: 87–98
- Irony: 88–90
- Logic: 94–120

Outlining

There are three types of outlining exercises. In the first type, students write the main idea and the supporting details for a single paragraph. These paragraphs are taken directly from the textbook stories. The use of textbook material makes the exercise more relevant to students and also reviews the stories. Students use complete sentences and proper indentation when writing the main idea and the supporting details.

The second type of outlining exercise gives students three main ideas from a story they have read. These main ideas provide a broad outline of the story. Students then write three or four supporting details for each main idea. Here is an example from lesson 21:

E OUTLINING

Complete the following outline for "The Spider, the Cave, and the Pottery Bowl" by writing the supporting details.

Copy each main idea; then write three supporting details for each main idea. Use complete sentences to write the supporting details.

1. *At the beginning of the story, Kate's grandmother was not normal.*
   a. Tell what she did most of the time.
   b. Tell what she no longer made.
   c. Tell how she seemed to feel.
2. *Kate and Johnny found some clay.*
   a. Tell where the clay was.
   b. Tell what kind of clay it was.
   c. Tell which animal was near the clay.

D RELEVANT INFORMATION

Write whether each item is **relevant** or **irrelevant** to the fact.

Fact: *The girl hammered a nail into a piece of wood.*

1. She had yellow hair.

   _____

2. She was building a doghouse.

   _____

3. She was putting a roof on a house.

   _____

4. Her dog was named Spot.

   _____

The third type of outlining exercise presents passages from the stories. Students write the main idea and the supporting details for each paragraph in the passage.

Relevant Information

Determining whether information is relevant to a fact is an important thinking skill. The relevant-information exercises teach students to identify which statements are relevant to a fact and which statements are irrelevant.

There are two types of relevant-information exercises. In the first type, students are given a fact and four statements. Students must identify which statements are relevant to the fact and which statements are irrelevant. Here is an example from lesson 26:

In the second type of relevant-information exercise, students are given two facts and four statements. They must then identify which statements are relevant to the first fact, which statements are relevant to the second fact, and which statements are irrelevant to both facts.

Contradictions

The contradictions exercises teach students how to identify contradictory statements in a text. There are three types of exercises. The first type presents a true statement and a contradictory statement. Students use an *if-then* statement to explain the contradiction. Here is an example from lesson 34:

D CONTRADICTIONS

Write the answer to item 1.

Assume this statement is true: *Libby loved all animals.* Then this statement is a contradiction: *Libby hated rats.*

1. Explain why the statement is a contradiction. Use this format: *If* ▬▬, *then* ▬▬.

In the second type of contradictions exercise, students are presented with a passage. One of the sentences in the passage is underlined. Students must find a sentence in the passage that contradicts the underlined sentence. Then they explain the contradiction in writing.

The third type of contradictions exercise also presents a passage, but without an underlined statement. Students identify the contradictory statements and then explain the contradiction in writing. Here is an example from lesson 40:

C CONTRADICTIONS

Read the passage below and find a statement that contradicts an earlier statement.

Many people are changing the way they eat. Rock star Biff Socko says, "I no longer eat any kind of bread. Bread is bad for you and hurts your voice." Every day, Biff has grapes and cucumbers for breakfast. Then he eats a large whole-wheat roll. He has been eating this way for a long time.

1. Underline the statement you assume to be true.

2. Circle the contradiction.

3. Write an *if-then* statement that explains the contradiction.

Figurative Language

Students in the program learn to recognize and interpret four types of figurative language: similes, metaphors, exaggeration, and sarcasm. Many of the exercises use examples of figurative language from the textbook stories. Each type of figurative language is taught separately.

Students first learn about similes. The initial similes exercise teaches students how to analyze a simile. Students identify which two things a simile compares and then explain how those things are the same. Here is an example from lesson 44:

E SIMILES

Write the answers.

The miner's hands looked like lumps of coal.

1. What two things are the same in that simile?
2. How could those things be the same?
3. Name two ways those things are different.

A subsequent similes exercise teaches students how to write their own similes. Students are given a literal statement such as *His heart had no feeling.* They then name something that has no feeling, such as iron. Finally, students use what they have named in order to write a simile, such as *His heart was like iron.*

The metaphor exercises are similar to the simile exercises. The students identify which two things are compared in a metaphor and then explain, in writing, how those two things are the same.

The exaggeration exercises teach students that exaggerations are statements that stretch the truth. Students identify which part of an exaggeration stretches the truth and then rewrite the statement so it doesn't stretch the truth. Here is an example from lesson 45:

D EXAGGERATION

Write the answers to items 1–4.

Exaggeration is another type of figurative language. When you exaggerate, you stretch the truth. You say that something is bigger or faster or longer than it really is.

Here's an example of exaggeration: *Frank worked for a year that afternoon.*

1. How long does the statement say Frank worked?
2. Could Frank really have worked that long in the afternoon?
3. What part of the statement stretches the truth?
4. Use accurate language to tell what the exaggeration means.

In the sarcasm exercises, students learn that sarcasm occurs when people say the opposite of what they really mean. The exercise presents a passage that contains a sarcastic statement. Students identify the sarcastic statement and then use evidence from the passage to explain what the statement really means.

Inferences

The ability to make inferences is essential for good reading comprehension. There are two types of inference exercises. The first type teaches students deductive logic, which is the basis of inference. In this exercise, students use rules and evidence to complete deductions. Here is an example from lesson 54:

D **DEDUCTIONS**

Write the answers for items 1 and 2.
   Here's the evidence: *All living things need water. An antelope is a living thing.*
1. What's the conclusion about an antelope?
   Here's the evidence: *Some birds cannot fly. An egret is a bird.*
2. What's the conclusion about an egret?

The second type of inference exercise requires students to apply what they have learned about deductions. The exercise presents an expository passage and a group of questions. Some of the questions can be answered by specific words in the passage. Other questions can only be answered by completing a deduction. Students indicate whether each question is answered by words in the passage or by a deduction.

Referents

Adult-level writing makes extensive use of pronouns and other referents that are often confusing to younger readers. The first type of referents exercise presents sentences that contain pronouns and adverbs. Students must identify the words to which the pronouns and adverbs refer.

Sometimes a word or phrase may stand for an entire sentence or a group of sentences. The second type of exercise teaches students how to interpret these referents. The exercise presents a passage in which a referent is highlighted. Students circle all the sentences the referent stands for. Then they write the main idea of those sentences. Here is an example from lesson 74:

C **REFERENTS**

Read the following passage and complete the items.
   Mesas are beautiful, but they have no water. The people must carry water from springs down below. They must carry everything they need. **It** is hard work.

1. Draw one circle around all the sentences that tell what *it* is.

2. Write a main idea that tells what *it* is.

   _____

   _____

Combined Sentences

These exercises teach students how to interpret sentences that use apposition. The first type of exercise presents a pair of sentences such as "The toucan has bright feathers. The toucan is a tropical bird." The first sentence introduces an unfamiliar word (*toucan*), and the other sentence tells what the word means. Students learn to combine the sentences to define the unfamiliar word: "The toucan, a tropical bird, has bright feathers."

In the second type of exercise, students read sentences that make use of apposition. Students identify both the appositive and the word it modifies. Here is an example from lesson 78:

B COMBINED SENTENCES

Write the answers about the combined sentence.

The limpkin, a brown water bird, has an unusual call.

1. What is the new word in the sentence?

   _____

2. What does the new word mean?

   _____

3. What else does the sentence say about the new word?

   _____

Following Directions

The following-directions exercises present a group of facts followed by a series of questions typically found on forms. Students use the facts to answer the questions. Here is an example from lesson 81:

D FOLLOWING DIRECTIONS

Use the facts below to answers items 1–4.

Facts: Your name is Homer Price. You are sixteen years old. You are applying for a job at a factory that makes doughnut machines. You know how the machines work, and you have fixed them before. You live at 417 Central Street in Centerburg, Ohio.

1. Write your full name, last name first.
2. What is your age?
3. Write your address, including street, city, and state.
4. List at least two qualifications you have for this job.

Reference Books

These exercises teach students how to use reference materials and how to read for specific information. In the first type of exercise, students learn the features of atlases, encyclopedias, and dictionaries. Students then identify which reference book they would use to find different kinds of information. Here is an example from lesson 85:

D REFERENCE BOOKS

Write the answers for items 1–6.

There are several kinds of reference books you can use to find information:

- A **dictionary** gives facts about words. It shows how to spell a word and how to pronounce it. It tells what part of speech a word is and what the word means. A dictionary also tells the history of words.
- An **atlas** gives facts about places. It contains maps of states, countries, and continents. It shows the distance from one place to another. It tells how many people live in each place.
- An **encyclopedia** gives facts about nearly everything. It tells about plants, planets, animals, agriculture, history, and famous people, among many other topics.

Which would be the best reference book for the following questions? Choose **dictionary, atlas,** or **encyclopedia.**

1. How do you spell the word *doughnut*?
2. How far is it from Denver to Kansas City?
3. What were the main events in Duke Ellington's life?
4. When did the Civil War take place?
5. How many people live in Mexico City?
6. How do you pronounce the word *succinct*?

The second type of exercise presents sample reference material. Students answer questions about the material.

Maps and Graphs

Students in the program receive extensive practice in interpreting maps and graphs. Maps appear in many of the stories, and questions about those maps are integrated with the story questions. In addition, there are two types of map exercises. The first type presents a map and a series of questions that involve direction, relative size, proximity, and interpretation of map legends.

The second type of exercise presents a map and a group of statements about the map. Students indicate whether the statements contradict the map. Here is an example from lesson 92:

C MAPS

Assume the following key and map are accurate. Examine the key and the map carefully and then read the statements in the next column. Some of the statements contradict what is shown on the map. Write **contradictory** for those statements. If the statement does not contradict the map, write **not contradictory**.

Key

- Cities in *italic type* have fewer than 100,000 people.

- Cities in **bold type** have between 100,000 and 500,000 people.

- Cities in **BOLD CAPITALS** have more than 500,000 people.

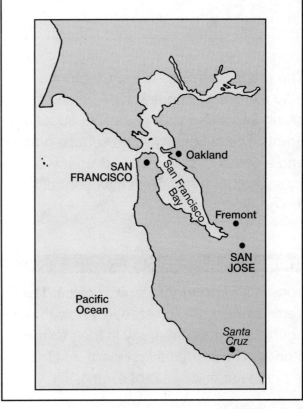

1. Oakland has more people than Santa Cruz.

_____

2. San Francisco is west of Oakland.

_____

3. Fremont is north of Oakland.

_____

4. Santa Cruz has more people than San Jose.

_____

5. San Jose has more people than Fremont.

_____

The graph exercises are similar to the map exercises. The first type presents a graph and a series of questions about the graph. The second type presents a graph and a series of statements. Students indicate whether the statements contradict the graph.

Irony

Irony is an important literary device. The irony exercises teach students how to recognize and interpret irony in their textbook stories. The students first learn that irony is the result of a chain of events.

- A character believes something.

- The character does things that are based on the belief.

- Later, the character finds out that the belief was mistaken.

The students then practice identifying this chain of events within stories they have read. For example, the story "The Necklace" tells about a woman named Matilda who loses a necklace she believes is valuable. She buys a new necklace and then spends ten years paying for it. At the end of the story, Matilda finds out that the original necklace was really a worthless fake.

Here is the irony exercise for "The Necklace," which appears in lesson 88:

E IRONY

Write the answers for items 1–3.
Here's how irony works:
- A character believes something.
- The character acts in a certain way because of his or her belief.
- Later, the character finds out the belief was mistaken.

Here's an example of irony from "The Necklace."
1. Matilda had a mistaken belief about the necklace. What was that belief?
2. Matilda did something because of her belief. What did she do?
3. What would Matilda have done if she had known the truth about the necklace?

Logic

In the last group of exercises, students learn seven rules for identifying logical fallacies. Each rule refutes a particular type of faulty argument. Here is a list of the rules.

• Just because two things happen around the same time doesn't mean one thing causes the other thing.

• Just because you know about a part doesn't mean you know about the whole thing.

• Just because a person is an expert in one field doesn't mean the person is an expert in another field.

• Just because the writer presents some choices doesn't mean that there are no other choices.

• Just because you know about the whole thing doesn't mean you know about every part.

• Just because two words sound the same doesn't mean they have the same meaning.

• Just because you know about one part doesn't mean you know about the other part.

The exercise for the first rule appears in lesson 94:

D LOGIC

Write the answers for items 1 and 2.

Here's one rule of logic: *Just because two events happen around the same time doesn't mean one event causes the other event.*

The following statement by a writer breaks that rule: "The last five times Sally tapped home plate, she hit a home run. She should always remember to tap home plate when she goes up to bat."

1. What two events happen around the same time?
2. What event does the writer think causes the home run?

The exercises for the remaining rules are similar. Another type of logic exercise presents several fallacious arguments. Students identify which rule each argument breaks.

Teaching Suggestions

Here are some suggestions for teaching the comprehension exercises.

Teach the exercises as indicated in the presentation book. New comprehension concepts are usually presented in a series of exercises that occur over several lessons. Students are then provided with practice in applying the concepts to different examples.

Monitor independent work performance. Students should be able to master each new concept within two or three lessons. If they don't, reteach the concept.

Reteach the concept to students who are having trouble. Repeat the exercises from the presentation book that teach the concept. Present individual turns to each student and reassign the exercises that appear in the textbook or workbook. Remind students they will be using the concept in later lessons.

Oral Reading

Oral reading occurs in every lesson of *Reading Mastery Plus,* Level 6. In the Before Reading segment of the lesson, students read word lists and vocabulary exercises aloud. In the Reading segment, students usually read part of a textbook selection aloud. In some lessons, they also read story background passages.

Story Background Passages

These passages present information about the setting, the characters, or the author of a story. This background information helps students understand the stories more fully.

You call on different students to read several sentences of the passage aloud. During this oral reading, you present the comprehension questions specified in the presentation book. (Suggestions for presenting these questions are discussed on page 43). Students should demonstrate a thorough understanding of the background passages because they will be using that information as they read the stories.

Textbook Selections

For the first twenty lessons of the program, students read the first part of every textbook selection aloud. Thereafter, depending on the group's decoding fluency, students can read the first part of some selections silently.

Oral reading begins with the title of the selection and continues to the diamond symbol. You call on different students to read two or three sentences each. Both during and after the reading, you present comprehension questions. (Suggestions for presenting these questions appear on page 43.)

In the first twenty lessons, the oral-reading segment has a decoding error limit, which is specified in the presentation book. The limit is based on the number of words to be read aloud.

- If students finish their oral reading **within** the error limit, have them read the remainder of the selection silently.

- If the group **exceeds** the error limit, students reread the oral-reading segment. Do not repeat the comprehension questions during the rereading.

Try to schedule the rereading as soon as possible. If there is time remaining in the scheduled period, start the rereading immediately. Students should not begin the silent reading and the independent work until they have read the oral-reading segment within the error limit.

Teaching Suggestions

Here are some suggestions for conducting oral reading.

Position yourself. If the group is large, circulate among the students as they read and observe their performance. Spend most of your time near students who need the most help, but move around enough to let all students know you are observing them.

Make sure you receive a frequent sample of each student's oral reading. Oral reading is especially important for students who are not fluent readers. If there are many students in your class, time may not permit you to call on each student to read every day. Make sure each student is called on every other day.

Do not call only on students who read well. All students should be given oral reading practice.

Do not overlook errors. During the first twenty lessons, make it clear to students that if they exceed the error limit, they must reread the first part of the lesson.

Respond to students' efforts as they are reading. Give them specific feedback from time to time, particularly if they are trying to read carefully. Tell readers who are reading fast and making errors to slow down. Encourage students who are guessing to read more carefully.

Make sure students follow along as others are reading. You can encourage students to follow along by asking them to listen for errors. They raise their hands when they hear an error. Students lose their turn to read if they don't have their place when called on.

Encourage less able students to point to the words that are being read. By pointing, students practice decoding throughout the group reading. If they do not point, they may practice only when they are reading aloud. Think of their pointing as a way of maximizing their practice.

Recognize and correct decoding errors. Here is a list of the most common errors:

- *Leaving off an ending.* Saying *look* for *looked* is an error. Saying *run* for *runs* is an error.

- *Saying the wrong word.* Saying *a* for *the* is an error. Saying *what* for *that* is an error.

- *Repeated self-corrections.* A self-correction occurs when a student says the wrong word and then rereads the word correctly. If a student self-corrects repeatedly, count each self-correction as an error. Occasional self-correction is not an error.

- *Word omissions or additions.* If a student frequently omits or adds words to sentences, count the omissions and additions as errors.

- *Repeated line-skipping.* Occasional line-skipping should not be treated as an error. Simply tell the student to move up to the appropriate line and reread the entire sentence. However, if line-skipping occurs frequently, count each occurrence as one error.

- *Repeated rereadings.* Occasional rereadings to fix the phrasing of a sentence are acceptable. Chronic rereadings, however, should be treated as an error. Count one error if a student frequently reads sentences in this manner: *They went with—went with—the boys from—the boys from town.*

- *Repeated word-part or syllable reading.* If a student almost always pronounces longer words a syllable at a time before saying the word, the student is making decoding errors. Count each chronic occurrence as one error.

Correcting Decoding Errors

Use the following procedure to correct decoding errors during oral reading:

1. Stop the student as soon as you hear the error. Do not wait for the student to finish the sentence.

2. Identify the error. Say, "You skipped a line" or "You left out a word" or "You repeated a word." For misidentified words, simply say the word and ask the student to repeat it. For example, say, "That word is *wizard.* What word?"

3. Tell the student to read the sentence from the beginning.

The last step is particularly important. If the student correctly reads the sentence in which the error occurred, the correction has been effectively communicated. If the student makes the same mistake or a different one while rereading the sentence, count the mistake as an additional error and repeat the correction procedure until the student reads the sentence correctly.

Working with Students Who Consistently Make Decoding Errors

Some students may consistently make decoding errors. Use the following procedures to help these students improve their oral reading.

Caution students to read carefully. Sometimes students have the impression they should read as fast as they can. Tell these students to slow down and read accurately.

Read long passages with individual students. Often, a student who is weak in decoding will tend to make a greater number of errors when reading long passages. You can take turns with the student. You read a few lines and then the student reads the next few lines.

Ask students to catch your deliberate mistakes. With this procedure, you read slowly and make mistakes from time to time. The student is to catch these mistakes. By reading slowly, you make it possible for students to follow along. By asking students to catch your mistakes, you encourage them to attend to the words even when they are not reading aloud.

Working with Good Readers

Many students in *Reading Mastery Plus,* Level 6, are proficient readers who make few decoding errors. You may determine that daily oral reading is not necessary for these students and decide to drop the oral-reading part of selected lessons. Nonetheless, these students should still read orally at least once a week.

Students who consistently finish their independent work before other students should be encouraged to read books and other print materials until the scheduled reading lesson is over.

Silent Reading

Students read the second part of each textbook selection silently. When students complete their silent reading, you present the comprehension questions specified in the presentation book. (Specific suggestions for presenting these questions appear on this page.)

Teaching Suggestions

Here are some ideas for helping students develop effective silent-reading strategies.

Watch students as they read. Make comments such as "Show me where you're reading. You're getting to an important part."

Remind students that you will ask them questions about what they read. Tell students they will be able to answer the questions if they read carefully.

Have students who finish early begin the writing assignment. These students should not begin any other exercises until after you present the final set of comprehension questions.

Occasionally, you may have to present the comprehension questions before every student has completed the silent reading. If so, students who have not finished reading should stop reading, listen to the comprehension questions, and then complete the silent reading later.

Comprehension Questions

You present comprehension questions during the oral reading and after the silent reading. These questions involve literal and inferential comprehension, sequencing, supporting evidence, cause and effect, and other comprehension concepts. There are also questions about character development, viewpoint, setting, plot, and theme.

The comprehension questions are specified in the presentation book and are always asked of individual students.

Teaching Suggestions

Here are some techniques for effectively presenting comprehension questions:

Ask the specified questions during the oral-reading segment. Do not wait until the end of the lesson to present the comprehension questions. Many questions involve predictions and other concepts that students should apply while they are reading, not afterward.

Add your own comprehension questions. If students have problems with a particular question, ask additional questions that will help them answer the original question. You should also answer students' questions—but don't become routinely sidetracked into long discussions. Nevertheless, reserve extra time for discussions of questions that are particularly interesting to students.

Accept all appropriate answers. Some questions require exact responses, but others can be answered in a variety of ways.

- For questions with exact answers, the student's response is preceded by the word *Response.* For example: Which is greater, the supply of Uncle Ulysses' doughnuts or the demand for doughnuts? (Response: *The supply.*)

- For questions with variable answers, the student's response is preceded by the word *Idea.* For these questions, accept any answers that express the correct idea, no matter what the phrasing. For example: How did Mr. Gabby think they could increase the demand for doughnuts? (Idea: *By advertising the doughnuts.*)

Correct errors immediately. When a student makes a mistake on a comprehension question, immediately indicate that the answer is not correct. Then call on another student to answer the question. If the second answer is incorrect, have all students find the specific sentence in the story that answers the question.

Present difficult questions twice. When a student makes a mistake on a difficult comprehension question, correct the error and mark the question in your presentation book. After you correct the error, say something like "I'm going to ask that question later, so remember the answer." At the end of the comprehension questions, present any questions you marked, along with any related questions.

Independent Work

As part of every lesson, students work independently in their workbooks and textbooks. They complete a wide range of activities in five main areas:

- vocabulary

- comprehension concepts

- story questions

- writing assignments

- reference and study skills

Most of the workbook and textbook exercises relate directly to the textbook selections. This direct relationship demonstrates to students that what they read is important and useful. When they do their independent work, students are rewarded for reading with good comprehension and for remembering what they read.

After students finish the textbook selection for a particular lesson, they *first* do the workbook exercises for that lesson. Students write the answers to workbook exercises in the workbook itself. When students have finished the workbook exercises, they complete the textbook exercises and the writing assignment on their own sheets of lined paper. They should write the lesson number and the name of the exercise and should number their responses according to the exercise numbering.

Students should *not* be permitted to look up answers in the textbook when they are doing their independent work. Although students develop "looking up" skills by using the textbook, the practice may prevent them from organizing and remembering information. For example, the independent work often requires students to arrange a list of story events in the correct order. Students who have trouble with these items may have an inadequate strategy for organizing events. You will not learn about their inadequate strategies, so as to help them develop better ones, if they are permitted to look up the answers.

Teaching Suggestions

You should monitor students as they work independently. Plan to observe them during the independent work for about five minutes each day and possibly for a longer period during the first twenty lessons. Walk around the classroom and observe students as they work.

First observe students you are most concerned about and identify any specific problems these students have. If a common problem emerges, such as misinterpreting an item, look at other students' papers. If many students are having the same problem, alert the class. For example, say, "Many students are not reading item six carefully." If only a few students are having the problem, plan to remedy it during the workcheck.

Here is a checklist for identifying independent work problems:

Are students skipping items? If so, say, "Check your work and make sure you have completed every item."

Are students reading items correctly? To answer correctly, students must first read the items correctly. Often it is possible to infer how a student misread an item from the student's answer. For example, one item asks "How was Homer related to Uncle Ulysses and Aunt Agnes?" Some students may answer "Yes." These students probably misread the item as "Was Homer related to Uncle Ulysses and Aunt Agnes?" Tell these students to read the item again.

Are students working without help? A major purpose of the workbook and textbook exercises is to develop students' ability to work independently. The more you help students, the less you know about how much they are learning, and the more they will rely on your help.

Are students working at a reasonable rate? Students who are not used to working independently often do not use their time well. To help students manage their time, tell them how much time has passed and how much time they have left.

Do students get stuck on a particular item? Students who have trouble with a particular item should complete their independent work and then return to the problem item. Tell these students to circle the problem item, complete the other items, and then return to the problem item.

Are their answers correct? If not, tell a student, for example, "Your answer to item five is not correct." Do not tell the student the answer.

Writing Assignments

Writing assignments occur at the end of every textbook lesson. Many of these assignments ask students to make judgments about important story events and to use evidence from the story to support their judgments. Other assignments encourage students to write about their personal responses to the selections. In still other assignments, students write their own stories and poems.

Lessons 1–10 include detailed instructions for presenting the writing assignments. In these lessons, you first read the assignment aloud and have students answer a series of questions related to the assignment. Then students complete the assignment by writing at least forty words. Finally, several students read their paragraphs aloud. You discuss with the class how well their paragraphs answer the assignment.

Questions or other prompts are included with all writing assignments. The questions help students organize their thoughts and check their completed assignments.

The minimum length of the writing assignments increases as students progress through the program. For lessons 1–10, the minimum length is forty words. By lesson 91, the minimum length is eighty words. Students should be encouraged to write as much as they want—the more words, the better.

Teaching Suggestions

Here are some suggestions for presenting and evaluating the writing assignments.

Evaluate according to content. The main point of the writing assignments is for students to get their thoughts on paper. Evaluations should be based on the content of the writing rather than the style. Focus on the ideas that students express and the evidence they present to support those ideas. Grammar and spelling should be attended to but should receive less emphasis.

Read examples of good writing. For every writing assignment, select a particularly good student essay and read it to the group. Explain what you like about the essay and invite students to comment.

Workchecks

The workcheck is a group activity. It should be conducted after students complete their independent work and before they begin the next lesson. Workchecks can be conducted right after the independent work, at another time during the day, or just before the next lesson. (The workcheck will be the opening event of the next lesson if students do their independent work as homework.) The workcheck takes about fifteen minutes.

The *Answer Key* contains reproductions of the workbook pages with answers written in. It also contains suggested answers for textbook exercises and criteria for evaluating the writing assignments.

During the workcheck, you first read the questions and answers for the workbook items, which are generally short. Students mark correct answers with a **C** and incorrect answers with an **X.** Then different students read their answers for the textbook activities. These answers are longer and more variable. You indicate whether each answer is correct. Finally, two or three students read their writing assignments aloud. You comment on each assignment and invite students to comment.

Teaching Suggestions

Here are some techniques for conducting effective workchecks.

Vary the workcheck procedures. Students may check their own papers during the workcheck, or they may trade papers, or you may want to check the papers yourself. The fastest procedure is for you to read each item and the correct answer to the group.

Keep moving ahead. If several students have questions about a particular item, tell them to mark the item with a question mark and explain that you will discuss the item later. Then move quickly to the next item.

Circulate among the students. Make sure they are marking each response. By circulating among the students, you will discourage them from changing their answers without first marking the items.

Give students time to correct their papers. Have them refer to the textbook selection and the glossary to correct their answers.

Count only some spelling errors. Spelling is corrected according to two simple rules.

- If the word appears in the question, it should be spelled correctly in the answer.

- If the word does *not* appear in the question, it should not be counted wrong if it is misspelled in the answer.

Accept variable responses for certain questions. Some questions can be answered in many different ways. For example, "Why did she go to the library?" can be answered with "To get a book" or "Because she wanted a book." Judge the answers to these questions according to the ideas they express, not by their literal wording. Do not, however, accept incomplete answers. In the example above, "a book" would be an incomplete answer.

Give general criteria for the writing assignments. Time may not permit you to read and comment on every student's writing assignment for every lesson. If not, review the general criteria for the writing assignment during the workcheck. Students can then evaluate their own writing. Do try, however, to give written comments to each student at least once a week.

Literature Anthology Stories

Each *Literature Anthology* story is accompanied by prereading activities and Extending Comprehension activities. The prereading activities include vocabulary words and definitions. In addition, the Story Background section provides information relevant to the story. Finally, Focus Questions help students track the ideas and themes of the story.

After the students read a *Literature Anthology* story, they are offered three different types of Extending Comprehension activities. These activities—Story Questions, Discussion Topics, and Writing Ideas—are often found in the broader language arts curriculum. You may choose to have the students do one, two, or all three of the activities, depending on the time available and the strengths and needs of your students. Look in the *Literature Guide* for more information about presenting and discussing the *Literature Anthology* stories.

Language Arts Guide

The *Language Arts Guide* contains teacher directions and blackline masters for daily language-arts worksheets. These worksheets focus on vocabulary development, figurative language, grammar, word parts, punctuation, and writing. They also provide students with exercises in using reference materials and developing and writing reports.

The worksheets from the *Language Arts Guide* can be presented at any time during the day, either to the entire class or to smaller groups of students. The exercises usually involve about five minutes of teacher instruction and an additional five to ten minutes of independent student work. Afterward, the worksheets should be checked. Use the procedures specified in the Workchecks section of this guide (page 46).

Program Reference Materials

This section contains a variety of reference materials for *Reading Mastery Plus,* Level 6, as follows:

- The Placement Test (page 50) measures the decoding and comprehension skills of students entering *Reading Mastery Plus,* Level 6. The test results provide guidelines for grouping students and also allow you to identify students who should not be placed in the program. Complete instructions for administering and scoring the Placement Test are included in *The Testing and Management Handbook.*

- The Scope and Sequence Chart (pages 52 and 53) offers a general overview of the concepts and strategies taught in the core textbook and workbook lessons for *Reading Mastery Plus,* Level 6.

- The Index of Skills for the *Language Arts Guide* (page 54) lists the skills taught in the *Language Arts Guide.*

- The Behavioral Objectives Chart (pages 56–66) gives a detailed explanation of each instructional track in the program, including the purpose of the track, the behavioral objective, the specific tasks the student performs, and the lesson range.

- The Skills Profile Folder (pages 67–76) summarizes the skills presented in *Reading Mastery Plus,* Level 6, and provides space for indicating when a student has mastered each skill.

- The Vocabulary List (pages 77–79) shows all the vocabulary words and phrases that are taught in the program.

- The Family Letters (pages 80–83) can be used with the families of students in the program. Letters appear in both English and Spanish.

- The Sample Lessons section (pages 84–111) includes a complete lesson from the presentation book, the textbook, and the workbook, as well as sample activities from the *Literature Anthology,* the *Literature Guide,* the *Language Arts Guide,* and *Activities across the Curriculum.*

Placement Test

Name _____

PART 1

The Golden Touch

Once upon a time in ancient Turkey there lived a rich king named Midas, who had a daughter named Marygold.

King Midas was very fond of gold. The only thing he loved more was his daughter. But the more Midas loved his daughter, the more he desired gold. He thought the best thing he could possibly do for his child would be to give her the largest pile of yellow, glistening coins that had ever been heaped together since the world began. So Midas gave all his thoughts and all his time to collecting gold.

When Midas gazed at the gold-tinted clouds of sunset, he wished they were real gold and that they could be herded into his strong box. When little Marygold ran to meet him with a bunch of buttercups and dandelions, he used to say, "Pooh, pooh, child. If these flowers were as golden as they look, they would be worth picking."

And yet, in his earlier days, before he had this insane desire for gold, Midas had shown a great love for flowers. He had planted a garden with the biggest and sweetest roses any person ever saw or smelled. These roses were still growing in the garden, as large, as lovely, and as fragrant as they were when Midas used to pass whole hours looking at them and inhaling their perfume. But now, if he looked at the flowers at all, it was only to calculate how much the garden would be worth if each of the rose petals was a thin plate of gold.

PART 2

1. *Circle the answer.* What kind of royal person was Midas?

   • an emperor   • a king   • a prince

2. *Circle the answer.* So his daughter was __.

   • an empress   • a queen   • a princess

3. What did Midas love most of all?

   _____

4. What did he love almost as much?

   _____

5. The more Midas loved _____,

   the more he desired _____.

6. Why did Midas think that dandelions were not worth picking?

   _____

7. What kind of flowers had Midas planted in his earlier days?

   _____

8. Midas used to inhale the _____ of those flowers.

9. What did Midas think about his garden now?

   _____

Scope and Sequence Chart for the Core Program

The following scope and sequence chart offers a general overview of the concepts and strategies taught in the core textbook and workbook lessons for *Reading Mastery Plus,* Level 6. The concepts and strategies are divided into four principal areas: decoding, comprehension, literature, and composition.

The colored bars show how frequently a concept or strategy is practiced, as follows:

- Blue bars show concepts or strategies that are practiced in **every** lesson.

- Green bars show concepts or strategies that are practiced in **most** lessons.

- Red bars show concepts or strategies that are practiced in **some** lessons.

The number at the beginning of each bar shows the lesson in which the concept or strategy is introduced. After introduction, all concepts and strategies are intermittently reviewed throughout the program.

CONCEPTS AND STRATEGIES

DECODING	reading words in lists
	reading aloud
	reading silently

COMPREHENSION:	comprehending vocabulary definitions
Vocabulary	using vocabulary words in context
	using context to predict word meaning
	completing crossword puzzles

COMPREHENSION:	answering literal questions
Literal Comprehension	recalling details and events
	following written directions
	identifying literal cause and effect
	sequencing narrative events

COMPREHENSION:	inferring causes and effects
Interpretive Comprehension	inferring details and events
	predicting narrative outcomes
	inferring main ideas
	inferring supporting details
	outlining

COMPREHENSION:	drawing conclusions
Reasoning	making comparisons
	evaluating problems and solutions
	identifying relevant evidence
	identifying contradictions
	completing written deductions
	identifying inferential questions
	identifying logical fallacies

LITERATURE:	interpreting characters' feelings
Literary Analysis	Identifying with characters
	interpreting characters' motives
	inferring characters' perspectives
	predicting characters' actions
	identifying characters' traits
	identifying settings' features

LITERATURE:	interpreting similes
Literary Devices	interpreting exaggeration
	interpreting metaphors
	interpreting sarcasm
	interpreting referents
	interpreting combined sentences
	interpreting irony

LITERATURE:	realistic fiction
Types of Literature	fantasy
	short stories
	factual articles
	novels
	poems
	biographies
	plays

COMPOSITION:	writing answers to questions
Writing	completing writing assignments

COMPOSITION:	interpreting maps
Reference	filling out forms
	using reference books
	interpreting graphs

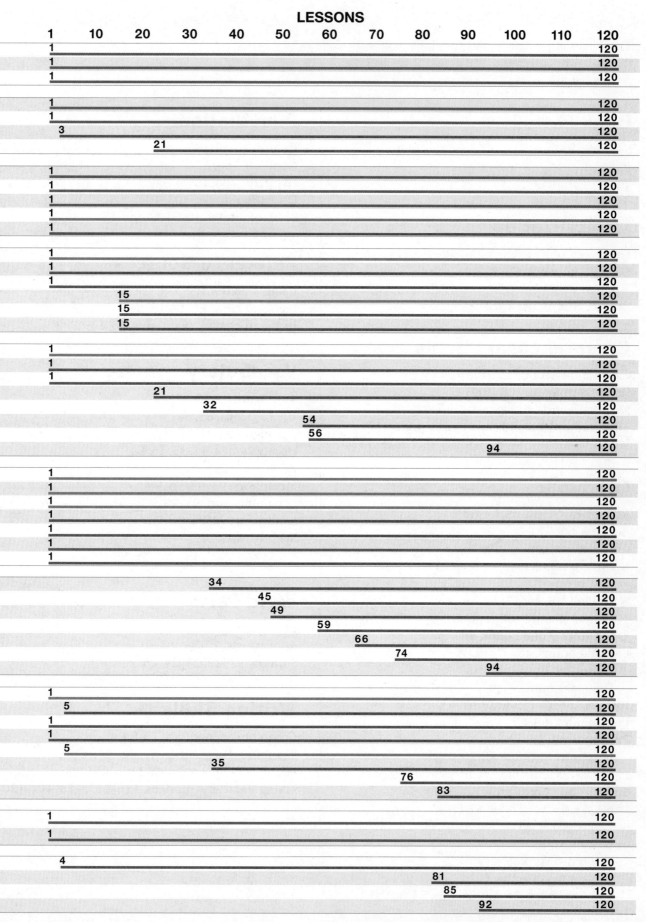

Index of Skills for the Language Arts Guide

The following index shows the skills taught in the *Language Arts Guide.* The numbers listed are lesson numbers.

Book Parts

Glossary, 3, 4
Index, 2, 4
Table of contents, 1, 4

Capitalization

First word of a sentence, 37, 39
Days of the week, 38, 39
Months, 38, 39
People, groups, places, languages, 37, 39

Comprehension Skills

Cause-and-effect relationships, 113
Fact and opinion, 108, 109
Location words and expressions, 111
Time and order words and expressions, 110
Words and expressions that signal change, 112

Grammar

Adjectives, 61, 62, 63, 64, 65, 67
Adverbs, 66, 67
Complete sentences, 40, 41
Complete subjects and predicates, 42, 43
Conjunctions, 70
Nouns, 44, 45, 46, 47, 48, 49, 50
    Common and proper nouns, 45
    Irregular plural nouns, 48
    Plural nouns, 46, 47, 48, 49
    Possessive nouns, 49, 50
    Singular nouns, 46
Parts of speech (review), 61, 63, 69, 71
Prepositions, 68, 69
Pronouns, 51, 52, 53
    Possessive pronouns, 52
    Pronouns and antecedents, 53
Subjects and predicates, 72, 73, 74
Verbs, 54, 55, 56, 57, 58, 59, 60
    Future-tense verbs, 58
    Linking verbs, 55
    Past-tense verbs, 57
    Present-tense verbs, 56
    Using verb tenses consistently, 59, 60

Punctuation

Colons, 101, 102
Commas, 75, 76, 77, 78
Hyphens, 106, 107
Quotation marks, 103, 104, 105
Semicolons, 99, 100, 102

Reference Sources

Using a dictionary, 5, 6, 7, 13
Using an atlas, 11, 12, 13
Using an encyclopedia, 8, 9, 10, 13

Vocabulary

Antonyms, 85, 87
Contractions, 83, 84
Homographs, 31, 32, 33,
Homophones, 34, 35, 36, 84
Idioms, 97, 98
Metaphors, 93, 94, 96, 98
Personification, 95, 96, 98
Similes, 91, 92, 94, 96, 98
Synonyms, 86, 87
Using context clues, 88, 89, 90

Word Parts

Prefixes, 14, 15, 16, 17, 18, 19, 20
Root words, 27, 28, 29, 30
Suffixes, 21, 22, 23, 24, 25, 26

Writing Skills

Combining sentences, 79, 80
Compound sentences, 81, 82
Fixing run-on sentences, 114, 115
Fixing unclear sentences, 116, 117, 118, 119, 120

Behavioral Objectives

The *Reading Mastery Plus* program is based on the concept that all children can learn if they are carefully taught. The program provides the kind of detailed instruction that is needed to teach basic reading, literature, and writing skills.

The sequence of skills in *Reading Mastery Plus,* Level 6, is controlled so that the student confidently performs the skills at each step before going on to more complicated tasks. The program builds on the skills developed in *Reading Mastery Plus,* Level 5, and also teaches new concepts in the following areas:

Comprehension—vocabulary; literal comprehension; interpretive comprehension; reasoning

Literature—literary analysis; literary devices; types of literature

Study Skills—writing; using reference materials

Activities across the Curriculum—science; social studies; math; writing; art

Language Arts—reading process; writing process

The Scope and Sequence chart on pages 52 and 53 provides a quick overview of *Reading Mastery Plus,* Level 6. The Behavioral Objectives chart on the following pages gives a comprehensive picture of *Reading Mastery Plus,* Level 6. The chart lists the various tracks (skills) that are taught and the range of lessons for each track. It focuses on both the general curriculum goals of the program and specific behavioral goals.

The chart gives detailed information about the skill tracks in the *Presentation Book,* the *Literature Anthology,* the *Activities across the Curriculum* project book, and the *Language Arts Guide.* The chart is divided into four columns:

- The **Purpose of the track** is the general curriculum objective.

- The **Behavioral Objective** is the kind of performance that can be expected from the student who has mastered the skill.

- The section headed **The student is asked to** describes the specific tasks the student performs in order to master the skill.

- The section headed **Lesson range** shows the numbers of the lessons in which the skill is taught or practiced.

Behavioral Objectives Chart

Purpose of the track	Behavioral objective	The student is asked to	Lesson range
DECODING SKILLS: WORDS To teach students to decode words	When presented with a list of vocabulary words, the student reads the list without error.	Orally read lists of vocabulary words.	1-120
	When presented with a list of hard words, the student reads the list without error.	Orally read a list of hard words without error.	1-8, 10-11, 13-16, 21, 25-40, 43, 45, 47, 52, 53, 55-57, 61-62, 74-77, 81-84, 86-95, 97, 99, 101, 104, 106, 108-116, 119
	When presented with a list of character names, the student reads the list without error.	Orally read a list of character names without error.	1-120
DECODING SKILLS: SENTENCES AND STORIES To teach students to decode sentences and stories	When presented with a reading selection, the student reads the selection aloud with a minimum of decoding errors.	Read part of a *Textbook* selection aloud.	1-39, 41, 46, 51-52, 55, 59, 61-62, 66, 71, 74-77, 81, 83-87, 89, 91, 96, 101, 106, 111, 116, 120 optional reading aloud 40, 42-45, 47-50, 53-54, 56-58, 63-65, 67-70, 72, 73, 79, 80, 82, 88, 90, 92-95, 97-100, 102-105, 107-110, 112-115, 117-119
	When presented with a reading selection, the student reads the selection silently.	Read part of a *Textbook* selection silently.	1-120
	When presented with a poem, the student memorizes it.	Memorize a poem.	51-52, 75-76
COMPREHENSION SKILLS: COMPREHENSION READINESS To prepare students for more advanced comprehension activities	When given oral directions, the student follows them.	Follow directions presented orally by the teacher.	1-120
COMPREHENSION SKILLS: VOCABULARY To teach students to comprehend vocabulary	When presented with a written definition of a vocabulary word, the student comprehends the definition.	Explain the meaning of a defined vocabulary word.	1-120
	When presented with a sentence containing a vocabulary word, the student uses context to define the word.	Define a vocabulary word based on context.	1-120
	When presented with a common word or phrase, the student explains what it means.	Explain the meaning of a common word or phrase used in a *Textbook* selection.	1-120
	When presented with vocabulary words representing dialect or accent, the student reads the words and tells what they mean.	Read and explain the meaning of words unique to a specific dialect or accent.	1-3, 30, 61-62

Behavioral Objectives (continued)

	When presented with a picture and a corresponding vocabulary word, the student describes the picture and defines the word.	Describe a picture and define a vocabulary word.	17-18
	When presented with a list of names of continents, the student reads the list and identifies each continent on a map.	Read a list of names of continents and identify each continent on a map.	21
	When presented with a vocabulary word, the student uses the word correctly in a sentence.	Use a vocabulary word correctly in a sentence.	1-120
	When presented with a crossword puzzle, the student completes it correctly.	Use vocabulary words to complete a crossword puzzle.	21, 37, 53, 91
	When presented with a homograph, the student pronounces and defines each word.	Pronounce and define homographs.	25
	When presented with a list of vocabulary words and a list of descriptors, the student uses classification skills to match the two lists.	Use classification to match vocabulary words and their descriptors.	24, 89
COMPREHENSION SKILLS: LITERAL COMPREHENSION To teach students to respond to literal comprehension questions when reading	When presented with literal questions about a reading selection, the student answers the questions.	Answer literal questions about a *Textbook* selection.	1-120
	After reading a selection, the student identifies literal causes and effects within the selection.	Answer questions about a *Textbook* selection by identifying causes and effects.	1-120
	After reading a selection, the student recalls or writes the main idea, details, and events from the selection.	Answer questions about a *Textbook* selection by recalling or writing the main idea, details, and events.	1-120
	After reading a story, the student puts events from the story in the correct order.	Put a list of events from a *Textbook* story in the correct order.	1-3, 7-8, 11, 14, 16-17, 23, 34, 35, 38, 46, 56, 71, 75, 81, 99, 102, 109, 112, 117
	When presented with written directions, the student follows the directions.	Follow written directions.	1-120
	When presented with a set of related facts, the student answers questions about the related facts.	Answer questions about related facts from a reading selection.	5, 22, 25
COMPREHENSION SKILLS: INTERPRETIVE COMPREHENSION To teach students to interpret what they read	While reading a story, the student predicts a possible story outcome.	Predict the outcome of a *Textbook* story.	1-120
	When presented with a story title, the student predicts the content of the story.	Use a *Textbook* story's title as a basis for predicting its content.	1-120
	After reading a selection, the student infers causes and effects within the selection.	Answer questions about a *Textbook* selection by inferring causes and effects.	1-120
	After reading a selection, the student infers details and events within the selection.	Answer questions about a *Textbook* selection by inferring details and events.	1-120
	After reading a selection, the student expresses personal reading preferences and feelings about the selection.	Express personal preferences and feelings about a reading selection.	1-120
	When presented with comparison items, the student makes comparisons by answering questions.	Answer questions by making comparisons.	11, 56, 57, 67-68, 107, 118
	When presented with a paragraph, the student infers the main idea of the paragraph.	Infer the main idea of a specific paragraph.	15-20, 23-24, 28, 35

Behavioral Objectives (continued)

	When presented with a paragraph and its main idea, the student infers details relevant to the main idea.	Infer details relevant to a specific main idea.	15-20, 23-24, 28, 35
	When presented with a passage containing two or more paragraphs, the student outlines the passage by specifying the main ideas and their supporting details.	Outline the main idea and supporting details of a specific passage.	19-22, 25-27, 30, 34, 38, 46, 58, 80-84, 116, 120
COMPREHENSION SKILLS: REASONING To teach students to use reasoning skills to respond to text	After reading a selection, the student draws conclusions based on evidence from the selection.	Answer questions about a *Textbook* selection by drawing conclusions.	1-120
	After reading a selection, the student evaluates problems and solutions within the selection.	Answer questions about a *Textbook* selection by evaluating problems and solutions.	1-120
	When presented with factual and fictional information within a selection, the student discriminates between fact and fiction.	Determine what information is factual and what information is fictional from a given selection.	4-13, 17
	When presented with statements and facts, the student determines which evidence is proof of a fact and which evidence is not proof of a fact.	Determine which statements are evidence of facts.	21–30
	When presented with facts and evidence, the student determines which evidence is relevant to each fact and which evidence is irrelevant.	Determine whether given evidence is relevant or irrelevant to given facts.	21, 23-30, 33, 35, 38, 43, 47, 61, 74
	After reading a story, the student uses reasoning skills to respond to a *focus question*.	Respond to a *focus question* related to a *Textbook* selection.	26-120
	When presented with a text containing contradictory sentences, the student identifies the contradictory sentences.	1. Explain how a given statement contradicts a given fact.	32-34
		2. Write sentences that contradict a true statement.	32
		3. Identify sentences in a text that contradict a given fact and then explain the contradiction.	35, 36
		4. Identify contradictory sentences in a text and then explain the contradiction.	37-42, 45, 65, 72, 85, 106
	When presented with the major and minor premises of a formal written deduction, the student completes the deduction by drawing a conclusion.	Write the conclusion for a formal written deduction.	54-58, 60-64, 97
	When presented with a group of questions about a text, the student distinguishes between the literal questions and the inferential questions.	Answer questions about a text and then indicate whether the answers came from specific words in the text (literal) or from inference (inferential).	56-60, 63, 66, 68, 76, 86, 102, 113
	When presented with a text containing a logical fallacy, the student identifies and explains the fallacy.	1. Learn seven rules for identifying logical fallacies, such as "Just because you know about a part doesn't mean you know about the whole thing."	94-120
		2. Explain how a given text breaks one of the rules.	94-120
		3. Identify which rule a given text breaks.	110-120
LITERARY SKILLS: ANALYZING CHARACTERS AND SETTINGS To teach students character traits and setting	After reading a story, the student interprets the feelings of a story character.	Answer questions about a *Textbook* story by interpreting a character's feelings.	1-120

Behavioral Objectives (continued)

	After reading a story, the student plays the role of a story character.	Answer questions about a *Textbook* story by pretending to be a story character.	1-120
	After reading a story, the student interprets the motives of a story character.	Answer questions about a story by interpreting a character's motives.	1-120
	After reading a story, the student infers the point of view of a story character.	Answer questions about a *Textbook* story by inferring a character's point of view.	1-120
	After reading a story, the student predicts the actions of a story character.	Answer questions about a *Textbook* story by predicting a character's actions.	1-120
	After reading a story, the student identifies the important traits of each story character.	Complete exercises matching characters with their traits.	1-4, 6-7, 11-12, 14-16, 19-22, 29, 31-32, 34, 37, 40, 44-45, 48, 51, 52, 54, 55, 57, 63, 66, 68, 74, 82, 83, 85, 89, 91, 94, 96, 97, 100-102, 113, 117
	After reading a story, the student identifies the perspective of a story character.	Answer questions about a *Textbook* story by interpreting a character's perspective.	9, 21, 25, 27-28, 30-31, 41-42, 49-50, 52-54, 59, 62-65, 95, 103, 104, 108, 110, 116, 119, 120
	After reading a story, the student identifies the important features of the setting.	Answer questions about a *Textbook* story by identifying the important features of the setting.	10, 14, 18, 28, 69, 79, 87, 105, 114, 117
LITERARY SKILLS: LITERARY DEVICES To teach students to interpret figurative language and other literary devices	When presented with a simile, the student explains what the simile means.	1. Identify which two things a given simile compares and then explain how those things are the same.	39-44, 46, 53, 62, 72, 84, 96
		2. Transform literal statements into similes.	47-50, 70, 78
		3. Identify similes within a given text.	57-60
	When presented with an exaggeration, the student explains what the exaggeration means.	1. Identify which part of a given exaggeration stretches the truth.	45-48, 69, 88, 108
		2. Rewrite a given exaggeration so that it does not stretch the truth.	45-48, 55, 69, 88, 108
		3. Identify the exaggerations within a given text.	57-60
	When presented with a metaphor, the student explains what the metaphor means.	1. Identify which two things a given metaphor compares and then explain how those two things are the same.	49-55, 67, 77, 107
		2. Identify metaphors within a given text.	57-60
	When presented with statements, the student identifies which statements are figurative and which are literal.	1. Identify figurative and literal statements.	43, 44
		2. Identify the type of figurative language used.	57, 59, 60
	When presented with sarcasm, the student explains what the sarcasm means.	Identify sarcastic statements within a given text and use evidence from the text to explain what the sarcasm means.	59-62, 71, 88
	When presented with incomplete lines using a specified rhyme scheme, the student completes the lines correctly.	Complete lines using a specified rhyme scheme.	51, 60, 67
	When presented with a spoonerism, the student rewrites it to make it correct.	Rewrite a spoonerism to make it correct.	55, 59, 70, 75, 103

	When presented with a lengthy dialogue in which the speakers are not always identified, the student identifies who says what.	1. Read descriptions of several characters and then identify which character might make a given statement.	61-64
		2. Identify the unnamed speaker for each line of an extended dialogue.	65-67, 79, 110
	When presented with a sentence containing pronouns or other referents, the student explains the meaning of each pronoun or referent.	1. Read individual sentences with referents and identify the person or thing to which each referent refers.	66-68, 73
		2. Read paragraphs with referents and identify the person or thing to which each referent refers.	71, 72
		3. Read paragraphs with referents, identify the person or thing to which each referent refers, and write the main idea related to the referent.	74, 75, 101
	When presented with a sentence that omits words, the student identifies the omitted words.	Identify words that have been omitted from a given sentence and then insert those words into the sentence.	69-73, 89
	When presented with a sentence containing an appositive, the student recognizes the appositive and explains its meaning.	1. Form a single sentence containing an appositive by combining two sentences.	74-78, 83, 104
		2. Form two sentences from a single sentence containing an appositive.	76-78, 86
		3. Insert an appositive into a given sentence.	79-83, 91
		4. Answer questions about a combined sentence.	115
	After reading a story, the student identifies and explains ironic situations in the story.	1. Recognize that literary irony occurs when a character acts on the basis of a mistaken belief.	88-90
		2. Explain given examples of literary irony.	88-93, 96, 102, 111
LITERARY SKILLS: TYPES OF LITERATURE To give students an opportunity to read a variety of types of literature	When presented with different types of literature, the student reads them.	Read the following types of literature:	
		fantasy	5-13, 22-25, 31-36
		factual articles	1, 4, 21, 26, 29, 31, 35, 36, 52, 61, 64, 74, 76, 87-90, 92, 97
		short stories	1-3, 14-20, 22-36, 52-59
		novels	4-13, 37-50, 62-73, 91-120
		biographies	76-82
		poetry	51, 60, 74, 75, 86
		plays	83-85
	When presented with the literary skill of repetition, the student explains the significance of repetition in the story.	Explain the use of repetition in a story.	3, 26-28
	When presented with a play, the student will work in small groups to perform the play.	Perform a play.	83-85
	When presented with a title page, the student answers questions about it.	Answer questions about a title page.	91

Behavioral Objectives (continued)

	When presented with various titles of previously read material, the student determines the type of literature of each.	Determine the type of literature of previously read material.	118
STUDY SKILLS: WRITING To teach students to integrate writing and reading	When presented with a written question, the student writes the correct answer.	Write the answers to questions presented in the *Textbook* and *Workbook*.	1-120
	When presented with a specific writing assignment, the student completes the assignment by writing a paragraph.	Complete writing assignments.	1-120
STUDY SKILLS: USING REFERENCE MATERIALS To teach students to use reference materials	When presented with a map, the student interprets it correctly.	1. Use a given map to answer questions about direction, relative size, proximity, labels, and other map-related concepts.	4-13, 15, 18, 21, 23, 26, 29, 36, 61, 66, 70, 73, 74, 76, 78-80, 87, 89, 90, 102
		2. Use a given map to determine whether statements are true or false.	91-95, 98, 99, 109
	When presented with a blank standard form, the student fills it out correctly.	Fill out standard forms.	81-84, 87, 103, 114
	When presented with the need for a reference source, the student identifies which reference source to consult.	Identify the appropriate use of atlases, dictionaries, and encyclopedias.	85-90, 94
	When presented with a graph, the student interprets it correctly.	1. Use a given graph to answer questions about quantity, change, and other graph-related concepts.	92-97
		2. Use a given graph to determine whether statements are true or false.	100, 101, 105, 115

Behavioral Objectives (continued)

Purpose of the track	Behavioral objective	The student is asked to	After lesson
LITERATURE ANTHOLOGY To elaborate on skills students are learning and provide a wide variety of literature	The student reads each story in the *Literature Anthology* and participates in activities related to it.	Read the following literature selections and participate in activities related to them:	
		Why Bush Cow and Elephant Are Bad Friends	10
		Blue Willow	20
		In the Middle of the Night	30
		The Shrinking of Treehorn	40
		The Gallant Tailor	50
		Shrewd Todie and Lyzer the Miser	60
		No One Is Going to Nashville	70
		Barn Gravity	80
		The Gold Cadillac	90
		The Hope Bakery	100
		Trick-or-Treating	110
		Willie and the Christmas Spruce	120

Activities across the Curriculum

Purpose of the track	Behavioral objective	The student is asked to	Lesson
ACTIVITIES ACROSS THE CURRICULUM To reinforce and extend concepts and skills acquired in *Reading Mastery Plus*, Level 6	When presented with a content area activity, the student completes the activity.	Solve math problems about rate and time.	5
		Compare a modern map with a historic map.	10
		Complete a chart	15
		Perform a scene from a story.	20
		Write directions for making a clay bowl and draw a picture of one of the steps.	20
		Rewrite sentences using more vivid language.	25
		Locate places on a map and write about those places.	30, 80, 105
		Explain onomatopoeia.	30
		Draw or paint a still-life picture.	30
		Perform a skit.	35
		Write a poem.	40
		Compare and contrast climates, novels and movies, and characters.	45, 50, 120
		Write a paragraph about air pollution and proposed solutions.	55

Behavioral Objectives (continued)

		Make a bar graph.	55
		Read a diagram to compare sizes of trees.	60
		Develop questions, conduct an interview, and write a news story.	65
		Develop a story map.	70, 75, 100, 110, 120
		Use a Venn diagram.	75
		Write lyrics to a song	75
		Write a letter.	80
		Make a recruitment poster.	85
		Write a dialogue.	85
		Engage in the choral reading of a poem.	90
		Write a description.	90, 115
		Calculate math story problems.	95
		Write a persuasive composition.	95
		Design a promotion poster.	100
		Participate in a mock trial.	110

Language Arts Guide

Purpose of the track	Behavioral objective	The student is asked to	Lesson range
LANGUAGE ARTS To teach students to use the reading process effectively	The student uses book parts to anticipate or predict content and purpose of a reading selection.	Answer questions and use a table of contents.	1, 4
		Answer questions and use an index.	2, 4
		Answer questions and use a glossary.	3, 4
	The student selects and uses a variety of appropriate reference materials.	Use a dictionary to answer questions.	5-7, 13-36
		Use an encyclopedia to answer questions.	8-10, 13
		Use an atlas to answer questions.	11-13
	The student uses simple strategies to determine meaning and increase vocabulary for reading, including the use of prefixes, suffixes, root words, contractions, homographs, homophones, antonyms, and synonyms.	Use the following affixes: dis	14-17, 19-20, 22, 24-28
		re	15-17, 19-20, 22, 24, 26, 28-30
		un	16-20, 22, 24, 25, 27-28
		pre	17, 19-20, 22, 24, 26-27, 29
		in	18-20, 22, 24, 27-30
		multi	19-20, 22, 28
		super	20, 22
		less	21, 23, 24, 26, 28
		ful	22-28
		ness	23-28
		er	24-27, 30

		able	25-27, 29, 30
		ible	25-26, 29, 30
		ly	26-28
		1. Use root words appropriately.	27-30
		2. Use the following Latin roots:	
		aud	29, 30
		cred	29, 30
		vis	29, 30
		dict	29, 30
		equi	30
		flec, flex	30
		port	30
		volv	30
		Use the following homographs appropriately:	
		light	31
		train	31
		tick	31
		down	31
		hail	31
		fast	31
		jar	31
		pen	32
		jet	32
		sock	32
		palm	32
		well	32
		lean	32
		stern	32
		top	32
		yard	33
		ring	33
		present	33
		Use the following homophone pairs correctly:	
		sea, see	34
		right, write	34
		board, bored	34
		feat, feet	34
		grate, great	34
		cereal, serial	34
		cell, sell	35
		fair, fare	35
		dew, due	35
		loan, lone	35
		coarse, course	35
		buy, by	35
		principal, principle	36
		hair, hare	36
		oar, ore	36
		plain, plane	36
		Identify and use contractions correctly.	83
		Identify and describe the difference between the following contractions and homophones: there, their, they're theirs, there's your, you're its, it's	84
		Identify and use antonyms.	85, 87
		Identify and use synonyms.	86, 87

Behavioral Objectives (continued)

	The student uses figurative language and other strategies to determine the meaning of reading material.	Use context clues to identify word meaning.	88-90
		Identify and explain similes.	91, 92, 94, 95
		Identify and explain metaphors.	93-95
		Identify and explain personification.	95
		Identify and explain idioms.	97, 98
	The student uses a variety of comprehension strategies to understand material.	Distinguish between fact and opinion in sentences.	108, 109
		Identify and explain the following: 1. time words 2. order words 3. location words 4. words signaling change 5. words that show cause and effect	110 110, 111 111 112 113
LANGUAGE ARTS To teach students to use the writing process	When presented with sentences and paragraphs, the student edits for correct capitalization, punctuation, and grammar.	Use capitalization correctly.	37-39
		Rewrite sentence fragments so they are complete sentences.	40, 41
		Rewrite sentences so they have correct subject-verb agreement.	72
		Use compound subjects correctly in sentences.	73
		Use compound predicates correctly in sentences.	74
		Rewrite two sentences as a compound sentence using correct grammar and punctuation.	79-82
		Rewrite run-on sentences.	114, 115
		Rewrite unclear sentences to make them clear.	116-120
		Identify the subject and predicate of a sentence.	42, 43
		Identify nouns, both common and proper, in sentences.	44, 45
		Identify singular and plural nouns in sentences.	46-49
		Identify possessive nouns in sentences.	49, 50
		Identify pronouns and referents in sentences.	51-53
		1. Identify verbs in sentences. 2. Use verb tense correctly in sentences.	54-58 59, 60
		Identify and use the following correctly in sentences: 1. adjectives 2. demonstrative adjectives 3. comparative and superlative adjectives 4. irregular comparative and superlative adjectives	61, 67 63 64 65
		Identify and use articles correctly in sentences.	62

		Identify a variety of parts of speech in a given sentence.	61-63, 66, 69, 71
		Identify and use adverbs correctly in sentences.	66, 67
		Identify and use the following correctly in sentences: 1. prepositions 2. prepositional phrases	 68 69
		Identify and use conjunctions correctly in sentences.	70
		Use commas correctly in the following situations: 1. words or phrases in a series 2. introductory words and direct address 3. dates, place names, and addresses	 75, 78 76, 78 77, 78
		Use semicolons correctly in sentences.	99, 100, 102
		Use colons correctly in sentences.	101, 102
		Use quotation marks correctly in sentences.	103-105
		Use hyphens correctly.	106, 107

Skills Profile Folder

Name _____

The following chart may be reproduced to make a skills profile folder for each student. The chart summarizes the skills presented in *Reading Mastery Plus,* Level 6, and provides space for indicating when a student has mastered each skill.

Reading Activities

Categories	Skills	Lesson Range	Date Mastered
DECODING SKILLS: WORDS	Orally reads lists of vocabulary words.	1-120	
	Orally reads a list of hard words without error.	1-8, 10-11, 13-16, 21, 25-40, 43, 45, 47, 52, 53, 55-57, 61-62, 74-77, 81-84, 86-95, 97, 99, 101, 104, 106, 108-116, 119	
	Orally reads a list of character names without error.	1-120	
DECODING SKILLS: SENTENCES AND STORIES	Reads part of a *Textbook* selection aloud.	1-39, 41, 46, 51-52, 55, 59, 61-62, 66, 71, 74-77, 81, 83-87, 89, 91, 96, 101, 106, 111, 116, 120 optional reading aloud 40, 42-45, 47-50, 53-54, 56-58, 63-65, 67-70, 72, 73, 79, 80, 82, 88, 90, 92-95, 97-100, 102-105, 107-110, 112-115, 117-119	
	Reads part of a *Textbook* selection silently.	1-120	
	Memorizes a poem.	51-52, 75-76	

Comprehension Activities

Categories	Skills	Lesson Range	Date Mastered
COMPREHENSION SKILLS: COMPREHENSION READINESS	Follows directions presented orally by the teacher.	1-120	
COMPREHENSION SKILLS: VOCABULARY	Explains the meaning of a defined vocabulary word.	1-120	
	Explains the meaning of a vocabulary word based on context.	1-120	
	Explains the meaning of a common word or phrase used in a *Textbook* selection.	1-120	
	Reads and defines words unique to a specific dialect or accent.	1-3, 30, 61-62	
	Describes a picture and defines a vocabulary word.	17-18	
	Reads a list of names of continents and identifies each continent on a map.	21	
	Uses a vocabulary word correctly within a sentence.	1-120	
	Uses vocabulary words to complete a crossword puzzle.	21, 37, 53, 91	
	Pronounces and defines homographs.	25	
	Uses classification to match vocabulary words and descriptors.	24, 89	

Comprehension Activities (continued)

COMPREHENSION SKILLS: LITERAL COMPREHENSION	Answers literal questions about a *Textbook* selection.	1-120	
	Answers questions about a *Textbook* selection by identifying causes and effects.	1-120	
	Answers questions about a *Textbook* selection by recalling or writing the main idea, details, and events.	1-120	
	Puts a list of events from a *Textbook* story in the correct order.	1-3, 7-8, 11, 14, 16-17, 23, 34, 35, 38, 46, 56, 71, 75, 81, 99, 102, 109, 112, 117	
	Follows written directions.	1-120	
	Answers questions about related facts from a reading selection.	5, 22, 25	
COMPREHENSION SKILLS: INTERPRETIVE COMPREHENSION	Predicts the outcome of a *Textbook* story.	1-120	
	Uses a *Textbook* story's title as a basis for predicting its content.	1-120	
	Answers questions about a *Textbook* selection by inferring causes and effects.	1-120	
	Answers questions about a *Textbook* selection by inferring details and events.	1-120	
	Expresses personal preferences and feelings about a reading selection.	1-120	
	Answers questions by making comparisons.	11, 56, 57, 67-68, 107, 118	
	Infers the main idea of a specific paragraph.	15-20, 23-24, 28, 35	
	Infers details relevant to a specific main idea.	15-20, 23-24, 28, 35	
	Outlines the main idea and supporting details of a specific passage.	19-22, 25-27, 30, 34, 38, 46, 58, 80-84, 116, 120	
COMPREHENSION SKILLS: REASONING	Answers questions about a *Textbook* selection by drawing conclusions.	1-120	
	Answers questions about a *Textbook* selection by evaluating problems and solutions.	1-120	
	Distinguishes factual information from fictional information in a given selection.	4-13, 17	
	Determines which statements are evidence of facts.	13	
	Determines whether given evidence is relevant or irrelevant to given facts.	21, 23-30, 33, 35, 38, 43, 47, 61, 74	
	Responds to a focus question related to a *Textbook* selection.	26-120	
	Explains how a given statement contradicts a given fact.	32-34	
	Writes sentences that contradict a true statement.	32	

Comprehension Activities (continued)

	Identifies sentences in a text that contradict a given fact and then explains the contradiction.	35, 36	
	Identifies contradictory sentences in a text and then explains the contradiction.	37-42, 45, 65, 72, 85, 106	
	Writes the conclusion for a formal written deduction.	54-58, 60-64, 97	
	Answers questions about a text and then indicates whether the answers came from specific words in the text (literal) or from inference (inferential).	56-60, 63, 66, 68, 76, 86, 102, 113	
	Learns seven rules for identifying logical fallacies, such as "Just because you know about a part doesn't mean you know about the whole thing."	94-120	
	Explains how a given text breaks one of the rules.	94-120	
	Identifies which rule a given text breaks.	110-120	

Literary Skills

Categories	Skills	Lesson Range	Date Mastered
LITERARY SKILLS: CHARACTERS AND SETTING	Answers questions about a *Textbook* story by interpreting a character's feelings.	1-120	
	Answers questions about a *Textbook* story by pretending to be a story character.	1-120	
	Answers questions about a story by interpreting a character's motives.	1-120	
	Answers questions about a *Textbook* story by inferring the character's point of view.	1-120	
	Answers questions about a *Textbook* story by predicting a character's actions.	1-120	
	Completes exercises matching characters with their traits.	1-4, 6-7, 11-12, 14-16, 19-22, 29, 31-32, 34, 37, 40, 44-45, 48, 51, 52, 54, 55, 57, 63, 66, 68, 74, 82, 83, 85, 89, 91, 94, 96, 97, 100-102, 113, 117	
	Answers questions about a *Textbook* story by interpreting a character's perspective.	9, 21, 25, 27-28, 30-31, 41-42, 49-50, 52-54, 59, 62-65, 95, 103, 104, 108, 110, 116, 119, 120	
	Answers questions about a *Textbook* story by identifying the important features of the story setting.	10, 14, 18, 28, 69, 79, 87, 105, 114, 117	
LITERARY SKILLS: LITERARY DEVICES	Identifies which two things a given simile compares and then explains how those things are the same.	39-44, 46, 53, 62, 72, 84, 96	

Literary Skills (continued)

	Transforms literal statements into similes.	47-50, 70, 78	
	Identifies similes in a given text.	57-60	
	Identifies which part of a given exaggeration stretches the truth.	45-48, 69, 88, 108	
	Rewrites a given exaggeration so that it does not stretch the truth.	45-48, 55, 69, 88, 108	
	Identifies the exaggerations in a given text.	57-60	
	Identifies which two things a given metaphor compares and then explains how those two things are the same.	49-55, 67, 77, 107	
	Identifies metaphors in a given text.	57-60	
	Identifies figurative and literal statements.	43, 44	
	Identifies the type of figurative language used.	57, 59, 60	
	Identifies sarcastic statements in a given text and uses evidence from the text to explain what the sarcasm means.	59-62, 71, 88	
	Completes lines using a specified rhyme scheme.	51, 60, 67	
	Rewrites a spoonerism to make it correct.	55, 59, 70, 75, 103	
	Reads descriptions of several characters and then identifies which character might make a given statement.	61-64	
	Identifies the unnamed speaker for each line of an extended dialogue.	65-67, 79, 110	
	Reads individual sentences with referents and identifies the person or thing to which each referent refers.	66-68, 73	
	Reads paragraphs with referents and identifies the person or thing to which each referent refers.	71, 72	
	Reads paragraphs with referents, identifies the person or thing to which each referent refers, and writes the main idea related to the referent.	74, 75, 101	
	Identifies which words have been omitted from a given sentence and then inserts those words in the sentence.	69-73, 89	
	Forms a single sentence containing an appositive by combining two sentences.	74-78, 83, 104	

Literary Skills (continued)

	Forms two sentences from a single sentence containing an appositive.	76-78, 86	
	Inserts an appositive into a given sentence.	79-83, 91	
	Answers questions about a combined sentence.	115	
	Recognizes that literary irony occurs when a character acts on the basis of a mistaken belief.	88-90	
	Explains given examples of literary irony.	88-93, 96	
LITERARY SKILLS: TYPES OF LITERATURE	Fantasy	5-13, 22-25, 31-36	
	Factual articles	1, 4, 21, 26, 29, 31, 35-36, 52, 61, 64, 74, 76, 87-90, 92, 97	
	Short stories	1-3, 14-20, 22-36, 52, 53, 54-56, 57-59	
	Novels	4-13, 37-50, 62-73, 91-120	
	Biographies	76-82	
	Poetry	51, 60, 74-75, 86	
	Plays	83-85	
	Explains the use of repetition in a story.	3, 26-28	
	Performs a play.	83-85	
	Answers questions about a title page.	91	
	Determines the type of literature of previously read material.	118	

Study Skills

Categories	Skills	Lesson Range	Date Mastered
STUDY SKILLS: WRITING	Writes the answers to questions presented in the *Textbook* and *Workbook*.	1-120	
	Completes writing assignments.	1-120	
STUDY SKILLS: USING REFERENCE MATERIAL	Uses a given map to answer questions about direction, relative size, proximity, labels, and other map-related concepts.	4-13, 15, 18, 21, 23, 26, 29, 36, 61, 66, 70, 73, 74, 76, 78-80, 87, 89, 90, 102	
	Uses a given map to determine whether statements are true or false.	91-95, 98, 99, 109	
	Fills out standard forms.	81-84, 87, 103, 114	
	Identifies the appropriate use of atlases, dictionaries, and encyclopedias.	85-90, 94	
	Uses a given graph to answer questions about quantity, change, and other graph-related concepts.	92-97	
	Uses a given graph to determine whether statements are true or false.	100, 101, 105, 115	

Language Arts Lessons

Categories	Skills	Lesson Range	Date Mastered
LANGUAGE ARTS: READING PROCESS	Answers questions about a table of contents; uses a table of contents.	1, 4	
	Answers questions about an index; uses an index.	2, 4	
	Answers questions about a glossary; uses a glossary.	3, 4	
	Uses a dictionary to answer questions.	5-7, 13-36	
	Uses an encyclopedia to answer questions.	8-10, 13	
	Uses an atlas to answer questions.	11-13	
	Uses the following affixes: dis re un pre in multi super less ful ness er able ible ly	 14-17, 19-20, 22, 24-28 15-17, 19-20, 22, 24, 26, 28-30 16-20, 22, 24, 25, 27-28 17, 19-20, 22, 24, 26-27, 29 18-20, 22, 24, 27-30 19-20, 22, 28 20, 22 21, 23, 24, 26, 28 22-28 23-28 24-27, 30 25-27, 29, 30 25-26, 29, 30 26-28	
	Uses root words appropriately.	27-30	
	Uses the following Latin roots: aud cred vis dict equi flec, flex port volv	 29, 30 29, 30 29, 30 29, 30 30 30 30 30	
	Uses the following homographs appropriately: light train tick down hail fast jar pen jet sock palm well lean stern top yard ring present	 31 31 31 31 31 31 31 32 32 32 32 32 32 32 33 33 33 33	

Language Arts Lessons (continued)

	Uses the following homophone pairs correctly: sea, see right, write board, bored feat, feet grate, great cereal, serial cell, sell fair, fare dew, due loan, lone coarse, course buy, by principal, principle hair, hare oar, ore plain, plane	34 34 34 34 34 34 35 35 35 35 35 35 36 36 36 36	
	Identifies and uses contractions correctly.	83	
	Identifies and describes the difference between the following contractions and homophones: there, their, they're theirs, there's your, you're its, it's	84	
	Identifies and uses antonyms.	85, 87	
	Identifies and uses synonyms.	86, 87	
	Uses context clues to identify word meaning.	88-90	
	Identifies and explains similes.	91, 92, 94, 95	
	Identifies and explains metaphors.	93-95	
	Identifies and explains personification.	95	
	Identifies and explains idioms.	97, 98	
	Distinguishes between fact and opinion in sentences.	108, 109	
	Identifies and explains the following: 1. time words 2. order words 3. location words 4. words signaling change 5. words that show cause and effect	110 110, 111 111 112 113	
LANGUAGE ARTS: WRITING PROCESS	Uses capitalization correctly.	37-39	
	Rewrites sentence fragments so they are complete sentences.	40, 41	
	Rewrites sentences so they have correct subject-verb agreement.	72	
	Uses compound subjects correctly in sentences.	73	
	Uses compound predicates correctly in sentences.	74	
	Rewrites two sentences as a compound sentence using correct grammar and punctuation.	79-82	

Language Arts Lessons (continued)

Rewrites run-on sentences.	114, 115	
Rewrites unclear sentences to make them clear.	116-120	
Identifies the subject and predicate of a sentence.	42, 43	
Identifies nouns, both common and proper, in sentences.	44, 45	
Identifies singular and plural nouns in sentences.	46-49	
Identifies possessive nouns in sentences.	49, 50	
Identifies pronouns and referents in sentences.	51-53	
Identifies verbs in sentences.	54-58	
Uses verb tense correctly in sentences.	59, 60	
Identifies and uses adjectives in sentences.	61, 67	
Identifies and uses demonstrative adjectives.	63	
Identifies and uses comparative and superlative adjectives.	64	
Identifies and uses irregular comparative and superlative adjectives.	65	
Identifies and uses articles correctly in sentences.	62	
Given sentences, identifies a variety of parts of speech in each sentence.	61-63, 66, 69, 71	
Identifies and uses adverbs correctly in sentences.	66, 67	
Identifies and uses prepositions correctly in sentences.	68	
Identifies and uses prepositional phrases correctly in sentences.	69	
Identifies and uses conjunctions correctly in sentences.	70	
Uses commas in words or phrases in a series correctly.	75, 78	
Uses commas with introductory words and direct address correctly.	76, 78	
Uses commas in dates, place names, and addresses correctly.	77, 78	
Uses semicolons correctly in sentences.	99, 100, 102	
Uses colons correctly in sentences.	101, 102	
Uses quotation marks correctly in sentences.	103-105	
Uses hyphens correctly in sentences.	106, 107	

Activities across the Curriculum

Categories	Skills	Lesson Range	Date Mastered
ACTIVITIES ACROSS THE CURRICULUM	Solves math problems about rate and time.	5, 95	
	Compares a modern map with a historic map.	10	
	Completes a chart.	15	
	Performs a scene from a story.	20	
	Writes directions for making a clay bowl and draws a picture of one of the steps.	20	
	Rewrites sentences using more vivid language.	25	
	Locates places on a map and writes about those places.	30, 80, 105	
	Explains onomatopoeia.	30	
	Draws or paints a still-life picture.	30	
	Performs a skit.	35	
	Writes a poem; writes song lyrics	40, 75	
	Compares and contrasts climates, novels and movies, and characters.	45, 50, 75, 120	
	Writes a paragraph about air pollution and proposed solutions.	55	
	Makes a bar graph.	55	
	Reads a diagram to compare sizes of trees.	60	
	Develops questions, conducts an interview, and writes a news story.	65	
	Develops a story map.	70, 75, 100, 110, 120	
	Writes a letter.	80	
	Designs a poster.	85, 100	
	Writes dialogue.	85	
	Participates in choral reading.	90	
	Writes a description.	90, 115	
	Writes a persuasive essay.	95	
	Participates in a mock trial.	110	

Literature Anthology

Categories	Skills	Lesson Range	Date Mastered
LITERATURE ANTHOLOGY	Reads the following literature selections and participates in activities related to them:		
	Why Bush Cow and Elephant Are Bad Friends	10	
	Blue Willow	20	
	In the Middle of the Night	30	
	The Shrinking of Treehorn	40	
	The Gallant Tailor	50	
	Shrewd Todie and Lyzer the Miser	60	
	No One Is Going to Nashville	70	
	Barn Gravity	80	
	The Gold Cadillac	90	
	The Hope Bakery	100	
	Trick-or-Treating	110	
	Willie and the Christmas Spruce	120	

Vocabulary List

The number following each word or phrase is the number of the lesson in which the word or phrase is first introduced.

abroad 25	bore 113	courteous 12	easel 30
absorbed 92	bough 57	craving 39	efface 51
absurd 43	box social 1	create a market 3	electrified 101
abuse 105	bricklebrit 24	crest 59	elude 112
accomplish 29	brim 92	crestfallen 102	emerge 36
accustomed 39	bronze 5	crimson 40	encounter 4
adopt 118	broth 29	critical 97	endure 53
adorn 37	bulky 89	croon 54	engaged 98
advanced 1	bungle 64	cross 16	enlarge 3
affair 16	burro 14	cubic inch 86	entice 33
aggravate 95	calamity 2	curlew 51	estimate 116
agitated 48	canvas 8	custom 11	eternity 109
agony 81	caress 48	dainty 27	ex- 50
agreeable 23	carpenter 7	day of reckoning 13	exception 84
ailment 95	casual 93	decayed 29	excessive 31
ambush 88	catastrophe 111	deception 82	exchange 24
amid 110	cavern 31	decked out 38	exhausted 25
anatomy 104	cease 6	deed 6	exquisite 34
ancestors 16	challenging 43	defy 66	famished 116
anguish 53	charter 110	delicacies 32	fasting 22
anon 60	chauffeur 1	demand 3	fawn 12
antic 102	cherish 7	departed 5	feeble 12
appeal 54	churn 63	dependable 26	fit 77
apprehensive 115	chute 2	deprive 23	flask 9
apt 33	citizens 3	deputy 113	flee 10
arouse 67	clad 117	despise 74	fleece 4
artificial 82	clasp 53	detain 35	flinch 112
assemble 23	climax 106	devoted 48	flirt 103
astound 84	clutter 110	devour 22	flustered 104
at rise 83	coffin 98	diameter 55	folly 104
atmosphere 105	collapse 25	diary 104	foolhardy 97
awe 40	collide 63	disaster 4	for a spell 1
bait 65	commotion 4	discard 39	forecastle 62
Bastille 40	complicate 66	distinct 109	forenoon 86
batter 1	compose 33	distinguished 38	forge ahead 72
bay 108	confidential 107	diversion 54	forlorn 40
bedraggled 44	congregation 94	divine 2	foster parent 57
bedstead 38	conscience 91	doth 60	foundry 118
beforehand 83	consent 111	doze 96	fragment 92
behold 33	considerable 95	drab 50	frail 37
best man 56	contemplate 93	dramatic 40	franc 52
bewildered 13	contempt 30	draw straws 5	fret 117
birch 59	contestant 55	drone 93	frivolous 34
blissful 109	coop 26	dryly 84	fulfill 5
bluff 117	core 56	dumbfounded 83	furnish 118
blunder 98	corral 14	dusky 12	gadget 2
boar 10	corridor 87	dwindle 89	gale 70

Vocabulary List (continued)

To the family of _____

   This school year your child is enrolled in the *Reading Mastery Plus* program. *Reading Mastery Plus,* Level 6, will help your child continue to develop the reading skills needed for success in school. This year your child will be reading well-known classics, such as *The Odyssey* and *Tom Sawyer,* short stories, several nonfiction articles, some poems, and a play. Many difficult vocabulary words are introduced in Level 6. Vocabulary exercises will help your child learn, review, remember, and use the words that are taught.

   Your child will learn study skills such as outlining, interpreting maps and graphs, and using references. These skills will help your child in other subject areas, such as science and social studies. In addition, your child will learn to recognize and understand relevant information, contradictions, figurative language, irony, and rules of logic.

   In *Reading Mastery Plus,* Level 6, your child will work on important writing and language arts skills. Research projects will require finding, reading, and using information to write reports. In other writing assignments, your child will apply information from the stories and articles read in the program.

   The best thing you can do this year is to let your child know that the work done in *Reading Mastery Plus,* Level 6, is important. Encourage your child to read something at home every day. Remind your child "the more you read, the better reader you will be."

   If you have any questions or want more ideas about how to help your child with reading this year, please call me at the school. I'll be happy to talk with you.

Thank you,

_____

A la familia de _____

Este año escolar, su hijo se ha inscrito en el programa de *Reading Mastery Plus.* *Reading Mastery Plus,* Nivel 6, ayudará a su hijo a seguir desarrollando las destrezas de lectura necesarias para triunfar en la escuela. Este año su hijo leerá obras clásicas muy conocidas, como *The Odyssey* y *Tom Sawyer,* cuentos cortos, varios artículos didácticos, algunos poemas y una drama. En el Nivel 6, se introducen muchos términos de vocabulario difíciles. Los ejercicios de vocabulario ayudarán a su hijo a aprender, repasar, recordar y usar las palabras que se enseñen.

Su hijo aprenderá destrezas de estudio como hacer un bosquejo, interpreetar mapas y gráficos, y usar materiales de consulta. Estas destrezas ayudarán a su hijo en otras materias, como ciencias y estudios sociales. Además, su hijo aprenderá a reconocer y comprender información relevante, contradicciones, lenguaje figurado, ironías y reglas de lógica.

En *Reading Mastery Plus,* Nivel 6, su hijo trabajará en destrezas importantes de escritura y lenguaje. Para los proyectos de investigación se requerirá buscar, leer y usar información para escribir informes. En otras tareas de escritura, su hijo aplicará información de los cuentos y artículos del programa.

Lo mejor que ustedes pueden hacer este año es comunicarle a su hijo que el trabajo que hagan en y *Reading Mastery Plus,* Nivel 6, es importante. Animen a su hijo a leer algo en la casa cada día. Recuérdenle que "mientras más lee, mejor lector será".

Si tienen preguntas o desean obtener más ideas para ayudar a su hijo con la lectura este año, por favor llámenme a la escuela. Me encantará hablar con ustedes.

Gracias,

_____

To the family of _____

    Your child has completed _____ lessons of *Reading Mastery Plus,* Level 6. Every day your child has worked on reading skills needed to achieve good grades in school. Your child can now read quickly and accurately. During this school term, your child has also learned many study skills and has gained an understanding of common types of figurative language, such as similes and metaphors. Your child can now find, read, and use information to write research reports. These are important skills that will lead to success next year in school and in all the years to come.

    During this break in the school year, encourage your child to read something every day. As in anything we attempt to learn, reading takes practice—lots of it. Remind your child "the more you read, the better reader you will be." Tell your child you are proud of the progress made in school.

    If you have any questions or want more ideas about how to help your child with reading during this break in the school year, please call me at the school. I'll be happy to talk with you.

Thank you,

_____

A la familia de _____

Su hijo ha completado _____ lecciones de *Reading Mastery Plus,* Nivel 6. Todos los días su hijo ha trabajado en las destrezas de lectura necesarias para sacar buenas notas en la escuela. Ahora su hijo puede leer rápida y precisamente. Durante este período escolar, su hijo también ha aprendido muchas destrezas de estudio y ha obtenido una comprensión de los tipos comunes de lenguaje figurado, como símiles y metáforas. Ahora su hijo puede buscar, leer y usar información para escribir informes de investigación. Éstas son destrezas importantes que lo ayudarán a triunfar en el próximo año escolar y en todos los años venideros.

Durante estas vacaciones escolares, animen a su hijo a leer algo cada día. Como en todo lo que intentamos aprender, la lectura requiere práctica—mucha práctica. Recuérdenle a su hijo que "mientras más lee, mejor lector será". Díganle a su hijo que están orgullosos de su progreso en la escuela.

Si tienen preguntas o desean obtener más ideas sobre cómo ayudar a su hijo con la lectura durante estas vacaciones del año escolar, por favor llámenme a la escuela. Me encantará hablar con ustedes.

Gracias,

_____

Sample Lessons

The following section contains sample lessons, exercises, and activities from *Reading Mastery Plus,* Level 6. Included are Lesson 37 from the *Presentation Book, Textbook,* and *Workbook;* the vocabulary and extending comprehension exercises for Story 2 from the *Literature Anthology* and *Literature Guide,* Lesson 60 from the *Language Arts Guide;* and Activity 13 from *Activities across the Curriculum.*

The examples in this section are of particular value to anyone learning to use *Reading Mastery Plus,* Level 6. An important part of learning to use the program involves rehearsal and practice. These samples give participants in staff-development sessions the opportunity to practice the procedures needed to organize and teach the lessons, exercises, and activities of the program.

Lesson 37

BEFORE READING

Have students find lesson 37, part A, in their textbooks.

EXERCISE 1

HARD WORDS

1. Look at column 1.
- These are hard words from your textbook stories.

1. **decorate**	4. **climate**
2. **bedstead**	5. **possession**
3. **tolerate**	

2. Word 1 is **decorate**. Everybody, what word? (Signal.) *Decorate.*
- (Repeat this procedure for every word in the column.)
3. Let's read the words again.
4. Word 1. Everybody, what word? (Signal.) *Decorate.*
- (Repeat this procedure for every word in the column.)
5. (Repeat the column until firm.)

EXERCISE 2

NEW VOCABULARY

1. Look at column 2.
- First we'll read the words in this column. Then we'll read their definitions.

1. **obliged**	4. **wardrobe**
2. **frail**	5. **adorn**
3. **plume**	6. **skylight**

2. Word 1. Everybody, what word? (Signal.) *Obliged.*
- (Repeat this procedure for every word in the column.)
3. (Repeat the column until firm.)

EXERCISE 3

VOCABULARY DEFINITIONS

1. Everybody, find part B. ✓
- These are definitions for the words you just read.
2. (For each word, call on a student to read the definition and the item. Then ask the student to complete the item.)

1. **obliged**—When you are *obliged* to do something, you are required to do it.
- What's another way of saying *She was required to visit Mrs. Jones*?
- What's the answer? (Response: *She was obliged to visit Mrs. Jones.*)

2. **frail**—Somebody who is *frail* is weak and delicate.
- What's another way of saying *The leaf was weak and delicate*?
- What's the answer? (Response: *The leaf was frail.*)

3. **plume**—A *plume* is a large feather. People sometimes wear plumes on hats.
- What do we call large feathers?
- What's the answer? (Response: *Plumes.*)

4. **wardrobe**—All the clothes you have are called your *wardrobe*.
- What is your wardrobe?
- What's the answer? (Idea: *All the clothes you have.*)

5. **adorn**—When you *adorn* something, you decorate it.
- What's another way of saying *Her hat was decorated with plumes*?
- What's the answer? (Response: *Her hat was adorned with plumes.*)

Lesson 37 **177**

6. **skylight**—A *skylight* is a window in the roof of a house.
   • What is a skylight?

• What's the answer? (Idea: *A window in the roof of a house.*)

CONTRADICTIONS

1. Everybody, turn to part E at the end of today's story. ✓
• (Call on individual students to read several sentences each.)
• (At the end of each section, present the questions for that section.)

Write the answers to items 1–3.
Here's how to find a contradiction in a passage:
• Assume that what the writer says first is true.
• Read until you find a contradiction.
• Make up an if-then statement that explains the contradiction.

• Name the three things you do to find a contradiction in a passage. (Idea: *Assume that what the writer says first is true; read until you find a contradiction; make up an if-then statement that explains the contradiction.*)

There are no underlined statements in the passage below. Read the passage and find a statement that contradicts an earlier statement.
   Bert was getting ready for his camping trip. At six in the morning, he started filling his backpack. He put in three shirts, an extra pair of pants, and some socks. When he left a few minutes later, the sunset was turning the sky red. Bert looked forward to his trip.
1. Write the statement you assume to be true.

• Which statement do you assume is true? (Response: *At six in the morning, he started filling his backpack.*)

2. Write the contradiction.

• Which statement is the contradiction? (Response: *When he left a few minutes later, the sunset was turning the sky red.*)

3. Write an if-then statement that explains the contradiction.

• What's the answer? (Idea: *If Bert left at six in the morning, then the sun couldn't be setting.*)
• You'll write the statement later.

READING

STORY BACKGROUND

1. Everybody, turn back to part C. ✓
2. (Call on individual students to read several sentences each.)
• (At the end of each section, present the questions for that section.)

The British Empire
In this lesson, you will begin reading the novel *Sara Crewe,* by Frances Hodgson Burnett. The novel takes place in London around 1880, and the main character is a girl named Sara. She attends a boarding school—a type of school where students live. Students stay at a boarding school all the time except for holidays, when they usually go home.

• What is the name of the main character? (Ideas: *Sara; Sara Crewe.*)
• What kind of school does Sara attend? (Response: *A boarding school.*)
• How is a boarding school different from a regular school? (Idea: *Students live there.*)

   Sara's father lives in India, where he is a captain in the British Army. At that time, India was a colony in the British Empire. It was one of many colonies around the world that were ruled from London by British kings and queens. The British Army stayed in India to keep control of the colony.
   Sara's mother is dead. Because Sara is a frail child who cannot tolerate the hot weather in India, her father decides to send her to boarding school in London. The map below shows the location of India and London.

- At the time of this story, what country was a colony in the British Empire? (Response: *India.*)
- Can anybody name other countries that were once colonies of the British Empire? (Ideas: *The United States; Canada; Australia; South Africa.*)
- Why were Sara and her father in India? (Idea: *Her father was in the British Army.*)
- Why did Sara's father return her to England? (Idea: *Sara could not tolerate the hot weather in India.*)

EXERCISE 6

FOCUS QUESTION

1. Everybody, find part D. ✓
- This is the title page for the novel.
  Sara Crewe
  by Frances Hodgson Burnett

- The picture shows a London neighborhood around 1880.
- Describe the houses. (Ideas: *They're connected; they look alike; they have skylights and chimneys.*)
- Why are there no cars? (Idea: *Cars hadn't been invented yet.*)
2. Now look at the next page.
- What's the focus question for today's lesson? (Response: *How did Sara feel about going to boarding school?*)

EXERCISE 7

READING ALOUD (OPTIONAL)

1. We're going to read aloud to the diamond.
- (Call on individual students to read several sentences each.)

CHAPTER 1
Miss Minchin
Focus Question: How did Sara feel about going to boarding school?

Miss Minchin lived in London. Her home was a large, dull, tall one in a large, dull square where all the houses were alike and all the sparrows were alike and where all the door knockers made the same heavy sound. On still days, the door knockers seemed to echo around the square.

On Miss Minchin's door was a brass plate with the following words:

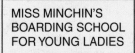

MISS MINCHIN'S
BOARDING SCHOOL
FOR YOUNG LADIES

When Sara Crewe was eight years old, she was brought to Miss Minchin's Boarding School. Her father, Captain Crewe, brought her all the way from India. Her mother had died when she was a baby, and her father had kept Sara with him as long as he could. Then, because the hot Indian climate was bad for Sara's health, he brought her to England to live in Miss Minchin's boarding school. Except for Sara, Captain Crewe did not have a relative in the world, so he was obliged to place her at a boarding school.

Sara was not a pretty child. She was thin, and she had a weird, interesting little face, short black hair, and very large green-gray eyes with heavy black lashes. ♦

EXERCISE 8

SILENT READING

1. Read the rest of the lesson to yourselves and be ready to answer some questions.

When Sara and her father came into the school, Miss Minchin took them into her office and said, "Sara is a beautiful and promising little girl, Captain Crewe. She will be a favorite pupil."

Miss Minchin was tall and had large, cold, fishy eyes and large, cold hands, which seemed fishy, too, because they were so damp. She touched Sara on the forehead, and chills ran down Sara's back as Miss Minchin repeated, "Yes, she will be a favorite pupil, quite a favorite pupil."

Captain Crewe was very sad at the thought of parting with his little girl. She was all he had left to remind him of her beautiful mother, whom he had dearly loved. He wanted his daughter to have everything the most fortunate little girl could have, so he took Sara out and bought her many beautiful clothes. ★

The saleswomen in the shops said, "Here is our very latest thing in hats. The plumes are exactly the same as those we sold to Lady Diana Sinclair yesterday." Captain Crewe immediately bought what was offered and paid whatever was asked. The result was that Sara had a most extraordinary wardrobe. Her dresses were silk and velvet. Her hats and bonnets were covered with bows and plumes. Her slips were adorned with real lace. Captain Crewe also bought her a large doll named Emily, whose dresses were as extraordinary as Sara's.

When they had finished shopping, they took a horse-drawn cab back to the school. Then Captain Crewe gave Miss Minchin some money and went away.

For several days, Sara would neither touch the doll nor her breakfast nor her dinner nor her tea and would do nothing but crouch in a small corner by the window and cry. She cried so much that she made herself ill. She was a strange child, with old-fashioned ways and strong feelings. She adored her father and could not believe that London and Miss Minchin were better for her than India. She had already begun to hate Miss Minchin and to think little of Miss Amelia, who was Miss Minchin's younger sister.

- How did Sara feel about going to boarding school? (Ideas: *She didn't like it; she cried about it; she couldn't believe that London was better than India.*)
- How many relatives did Sara's father have besides Sara? (Idea: *None.*)

- What was the name of the boarding school Sara went to? (Response: *Miss Minchin's Boarding School for Young Ladies.*)
- Tell three things about Sara when she first came to the boarding school. (Ideas: *She was eight years old; she was not a pretty child; she had nice clothes; she was sad to be there; she was not very healthy.*)
- Tell three things about Miss Minchin. (Ideas: *She was tall and big; she had fishy eyes; she had cold, wet hands.*)
- Why did Captain Crewe buy Sara so many clothes? (Idea: *He wanted her to have everything a fortunate girl should have.*)
- What did Sara do for several days after her father left? (Ideas: *Didn't eat; crouched in a corner and cried; made herself ill.*)
- How did Sara feel about Miss Minchin? (Idea: *She hated her.*)

EXERCISE 9

PAIRED PRACTICE (OPTIONAL)

1. Now you'll read in pairs.
- Whoever read second the last time will read first today.
- Remember to start at the diamond and switch at the star.
2. (Observe students and answer questions as needed.)

AFTER READING

EXERCISE 10

INDEPENDENT WORK

1. Do all the items in your workbook and textbook for this lesson.
2. (The independent work in this lesson includes the following activities.)
- Story details
- Vocabulary
- Crossword puzzle
- Character traits
- Contradictions
- Vocabulary review
- Comprehension
- Writing

180 *Lesson 37*

WORKCHECK

1. (Using the Answer Key, read the questions and answers for the workbook.)
2. (Have students read their answers for the textbook activities.)
3. (Have two or three students read their writing assignments aloud. Comment on each assignment.)
4. (Have students correct and turn in their work.)

(Students should complete the appropriate exercises in the *Language Arts Guide* after completing lesson 37. See *Language Arts Guide* for details.)

A WORD LISTS

1
Hard Words
1. decorate
2. bedstead
3. tolerate
4. climate
5. possession

2
New Vocabulary
1. obliged
2. frail
3. plume
4. wardrobe
5. adorn
6. skylight

B VOCABULARY DEFINITIONS

1. **obliged**—When you are *obliged* to do something, you are required to do it.
   • What's another way of saying *She was required to visit Mrs. Jones*?

2. **frail**—Somebody who is *frail* is weak and delicate.
   • What's another way of saying *The leaf was weak and delicate*?

3. **plume**—A *plume* is a large feather. People sometimes wear plumes on hats.
   • What do we call large feathers?

4. **wardrobe**—All the clothes you have are called your *wardrobe*.
   • What is your wardrobe?

5. **adorn**—When you *adorn* something, you decorate it.
   • What's another way of saying *Her hat was decorated with plumes*?

6. **skylight**—A *skylight* is a window in the roof of a house.
   • What is a skylight?

STORY BACKGROUND

The British Empire

In this lesson, you will begin reading the novel *Sara Crewe*, by Frances Hodgson Burnett. The novel takes place in London around 1880, and the main character is a girl named Sara. She attends a boarding school—a type of school where students live. Students stay at a boarding school all the time except for holidays, when they usually go home.

Sara's father lives in India, where he is a captain in the British Army. At that time,

India was a colony in the British Empire. It was one of many colonies around the world that were ruled from London by British kings and queens. The British Army stayed in India to keep control of the colony.

Sara's mother is dead. Because Sara is a frail child who cannot tolerate the hot weather in India, her father decides to send her to boarding school in London. The map below shows the location of India and London.

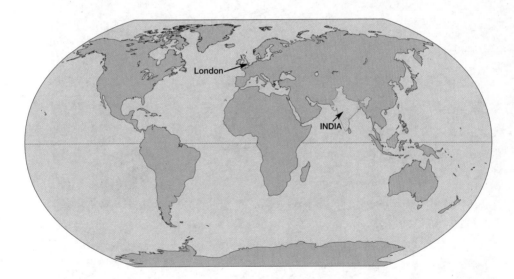

D READING

Sara Crewe
by Frances Hodgson Burnett*

* Adapted for young readers

Chapter 1
Miss Minchin

Focus Question: How did Sara feel about going to boarding school?

Miss Minchin lived in London. Her home was a large, dull, tall one in a large, dull square where all the houses were alike and all the sparrows were alike and where all the door knockers made the same heavy sound. On still days, the door knockers seemed to echo around the square.

On Miss Minchin's door was a brass plate with the following words:

> MISS MINCHIN'S
> BOARDING SCHOOL
> FOR YOUNG LADIES

When Sara Crewe was eight years old, she was brought to Miss Minchin's Boarding School. Her father, Captain Crewe, brought her all the way from India. Her mother had died when she was a baby, and her father had kept Sara with him as long as he could. Then, because the hot Indian climate was bad for Sara's health, he brought her to England to live in Miss Minchin's boarding school. Except for Sara, Captain Crewe did not have a relative in the world, so he was obliged to place her at a boarding school.

Sara was not a pretty child. She was thin, and she had a weird, interesting little face, short black hair, and very large green-gray eyes with heavy black lashes.♦

When Sara and her father came into the school, Miss Minchin took them into her office and said, "Sara is a beautiful and promising little girl, Captain Crewe. She will be a favorite pupil."

Miss Minchin was tall and had large, cold, fishy eyes and large, cold hands, which seemed fishy, too, because they were so damp. She touched Sara on the forehead, and chills ran down Sara's back as Miss Minchin repeated, "Yes, she will be a favorite pupil, quite a favorite pupil."

Captain Crewe was very sad at the thought of parting with his little girl. She was all he had left to remind him of her beautiful mother, whom he had dearly loved. He wanted his daughter to have everything the most fortunate little girl could have, so he took Sara out and bought her many beautiful clothes. ★

The saleswomen in the shops said, "Here is our very latest thing in hats. The plumes are exactly the same as those we sold to Lady Diana Sinclair yesterday." Captain Crewe immediately bought what was offered and paid whatever was asked. The result was that Sara had a most extraordinary wardrobe. Her dresses were silk and velvet. Her hats and bonnets were covered with bows and plumes. Her slips were adorned with real lace. Captain Crewe also bought her a large doll named Emily, whose dresses were as extraordinary as Sara's.

When they had finished shopping, they took a horse-drawn cab back to the school. Then Captain Crewe gave Miss Minchin some money and went away.

For several days, Sara would neither touch the doll nor her breakfast nor her dinner nor her tea and would do nothing but crouch in a small corner by the window and cry. She cried so much that she made herself ill. She was a strange child, with old-fashioned ways and strong feelings. She adored her father and could not believe that London and Miss Minchin were better for her than India. She had already begun to hate Miss Minchin and to think little of Miss Amelia, who was Miss Minchin's younger sister.

E CONTRADICTIONS

Write the answers to items 1–3.

Here's how to find a contradiction in a passage:

- Assume that what the writer says first is true.
- Read until you find a contradiction.
- Make up an if-then statement that explains the contradiction.

There are no underlined statements in the passage below. Read the passage and find a statement that contradicts an earlier statement.

Bert was getting ready for his camping trip. At six in the morning, he started filling his backpack. He put in three shirts, an extra pair of pants, and some socks. When he left a few minutes later, the sunset was turning the sky red. Bert looked forward to his trip.

1. Write the statement you assume to be true.
2. Write the contradiction.
3. Write an if-then statement that explains the contradiction.

F VOCABULARY REVIEW

detain
gratifying
lush
liberty
emerges

For each item, write the correct word.
1. Plants that are growing well are ▮▮▮.
2. When something comes out of a place, it ▮▮▮ from that place.
3. Another word for *freedom* is ▮▮▮.

G COMPREHENSION

Write the answers.
1. How did Sara feel about going to boarding school?
2. How is a boarding school different from a regular school?
3. In what ways was Miss Minchin like a fish?
4. Why did Captain Crewe buy Sara such extraordinary clothes?
5. Why did Sara have to leave India?

H WRITING

What kind of school would you rather go to, a boarding school or a regular school?

Write an essay that explains what kind of school you would prefer. Try to answer the following questions:
- In what ways are boarding schools better than regular schools?
- In what ways are regular schools better than boarding schools?
- Which type of school would you prefer? Why?

Make your essay at least fifty words long.

37

Name_____

<table>
<tr><td>

A STORY DETAILS

Write or circle the answers.

1. In what city did Miss Minchin live?

   _____

2. What country had Sara come from?

   _____

3. What was the weather like in that
   country?

   _____

4. What kind of school did Miss Minchin
   run?

   _____

5. How old was Sara when she arrived at
   Miss Minchin's school?

   _____

6. Captain Crewe bought Sara some __
   clothes.

   • practical   • inexpensive   • exquisite

7. What materials were Sara's new dresses
   made of?

   _____

8. What toy did Captain Crewe buy for
   Sara?

   _____

</td><td>

B VOCABULARY

Write the correct words in the blanks.

indignant	exquisite
lush	accord
detain	emerged
recollect	liberty
frivolous	gratifying

1. It took months to make this

   _____ silk dress.

2. The girl could not _____
   where she left her doll.

3. The bad cook was _____
   about his customers' complaints.

4. The prisoners went into the yard of their

   own _____.

5. The reporters tried to _____
   her to ask more questions.

6. The deer lay down in the _____
   meadow.

7. One great man said, "Give me

   _____ or give me death!"

8. The groundhog _____ from
   his hole and took a look around.

9. After all our hard work, their praise was

   _____.

</td></tr>
</table>

C CROSSWORD PUZZLE

Use the clues to complete the puzzle.

Across

1. Someone who is wise and careful is ＿.

2. A person's reason for doing something is the person's ＿.

3. When you are angry and insulted, you are ＿.

5. When you delay somebody, you ＿ that person.

7. Another word for *sad*

9. Another word for *foolish*

Down

1. A red fruit that contains many seeds

4. Something that is very high is ＿.

6. A bit of food is a ＿.

8. Plants that have lots of leaves are ＿.

D CHARACTER TRAITS

Write which character each phrase or statement describes. Choose **Miss Minchin, Sara,** or **Captain Crewe.**

1. An officer in the army

   _____

2. Was like a fish

   _____

3. His wife had died.

   _____

4. Had an extraordinary wardrobe

   _____

5. Ran a school

   _____

■■GO TO PART E IN YOUR TEXTBOOK.■■

BLUE WILLOW

by Pam Conrad
Illustrated by S. Saelig Gallagher

New Vocabulary Words

1. merchant
2. scroll
3. pavilion

4. embroider
5. lute
6. reluctance

7. turmoil
8. topple
9. commission
10. heed

Definitions

1. A **merchant** is a person who buys and sells things.
2. A **scroll** is a long piece of fine paper or silk that people write on. A scroll is rolled up when not in use.
3. A **pavilion** is an open building where you can sit to watch a performance or observe nature.
4. When you **embroider,** you sew designs on a cloth.
5. A **lute** is a stringed musical instrument that has an egg-shaped guitar body with the very top part bent back.
6. When you do something with **reluctance,** you do it unwillingly and without enthusiasm.
7. **Turmoil** is another way of saying *chaos and confusion.*
8. When things or people **topple,** they fall over.
9. When you **commission** a piece of art, you pay the artist to make the piece of art the way you want it designed.
10. When you **heed** what someone tells you, you pay attention and listen to what is said.

Story Background

"Blue Willow" is Pam Conrad's personal interpretation of a Chinese legend. She learned about the legend from a Blue Willow plate that was in her family. Blue Willow plates were first made in England during the 1700s, when British culture was greatly influenced by Chinese culture. The pattern on the plates became very popular in England and America. Blue Willow plates are still made and collected today. The legend was inspired by the beautiful pattern. As is typical of legends, there are many versions, but the basic ingredients remain the same.

Pam Conrad wrote her version of the Blue Willow legend when her daughter grew up and fell in love. Pam Conrad's message is one for all parents: Listen to your children and take them seriously when they speak to you about matters of the heart.

Much of this legend takes place outdoors. Here are some words particular to this setting that will help you understand and enjoy the story. **Peonies** and **orchids** are flowers known for their beautiful blossoms. **Cassias** and **willows** are types of trees. **Sandpipers** and

16

cormorants are birds that are found near water. **Cicadas** are insects that make loud, shrill sounds.

Water plays an important role in this legend. **Monsoons** are seasonal winds that bring very heavy rains that often result in flooding. **Monsoon rains** can be described as **torrential** because so much water comes down. Other words that describe this intense movement of water are **surging** and **churning.**

Jewelry also has a part in this legend. Since Kung Shi Fair is the daughter of a wealthy man, she is used to the finest jewelry made of gold. Gold can be described as **lustrous** because of its luster, or shiny quality. **Trinkets** are cheap jewelry of little or no monetary value. For Kung Shi Fair, trinkets are made of **jade,** a green-colored mineral; of **ivory,** from animal tusks; or of **brass,** an inexpensive metal.

Chang the Good, the young man whom Kung Shi Fair wants to marry, brings her a variety of trinkets as a sign of his affection. To Chang, these are his most precious treasures, as they had belonged to his mother, who died when he was young. In a simple bundle, he brings necklaces, pendants (necklaces with jewels hanging from them), and bracelets, along with brooches to pin on Kung Shi Fair's clothing.

Focus Questions

- Why is Kung Shi Fair's father reluctant to give his daughter the one thing she wants from him?
- Because they love each other, what do Kung Shi Fair and Chang the Good do during the raging storm?
- What lesson does the wealthy merchant learn, and what does he do so others might benefit from his mistakes?

(The story "Blue Willow" begins at this point in the *Literature Anthology*.)

17

Extending Comprehension

Story Questions

1. In what ways does Kung Shi Fair's father spoil her?
2. Where and how do Chang and Kung Shi Fair meet?
3. What is the terrible news delivered by one of the merchant's servants?
4. What are the different ways the merchant puts off his daughter's most important request?
5. How does Chang react to the merchant's reluctance?
6. What do the villagers decide to do, in spite of the raging storm?
7. Why doesn't Chang join the villagers? Where does he go instead?
8. What does Chang realize when his cormorant brings him something other than a fish from the water?
9. Where does Kung Shi Fair go during the storm and why?
10. After almost giving up on finding the leopard, the villagers hear a sound. What happens next?
11. What do the villagers later figure out about the sound?
12. What does the merchant do so his daughter and Chang the Good are never forgotten?
13. What lesson does the merchant learn?

Discussion Topics

1. Do you think there was a leopard rampaging through the village? How might the legend be different if there hadn't been a leopard? During your discussion, try to answer the following questions:

   - Why do you think a leopard is included as part of the legend?
   - What evidence suggests there was a leopard?
   - What evidence suggests there might not have been a leopard?

2. Water is like a character in this legend. What are some of the important roles that water plays? During your discussion, try to answer the following questions:

   - What different events take place on the river?
   - What happens because of the torrential rains?
   - Could there have been a rainbow over the stone bridge without water?

3. This legend has a tragic ending. How could the deaths of the main characters been avoided? During your discussion, try to answer the following questions:

   - Why didn't Kung Shi Fair know how to use her boat?
   - Why didn't Chang the Good go on the leopard hunt with the other villagers?
   - How are the three villagers feeling as they jump into their boats to go kill the leopard?
   - If Kung Shi Fair's father had agreed to let his daughter marry Chang the Good, would the couple have behaved differently the night of the storm?

4. If you have access to the Internet, go to the following Web site:
   www.willowcollectors.org/legend.html.
   On the Web site, there is a poem about the Blue Willow legend. Read it aloud. Discuss the similarities and differences between the poem and the story you read.

36

Writing Ideas

1. Chang is a clever young man. For example, he trains his cormorant to bring fish back to him. Write a letter to Kung Shi Fair's father explaining why Chang is a worthy husband for his daughter.

2. The author uses figurative language, specifically similes, to describe the sound Chang makes when he learns of Kung Shi's death. These examples include: "like the sound of a trapped animal just before it dies" and "like the ragings of a rampaging leopard before it strikes."

   Try to imagine the sound Chang made at that terrible moment and write two of your own similes to describe what you hear. Then try to imagine Kung Shi's fear and horror as the hull of her boat snapped apart and she was pulled into the surging river. Write two more similes to describe Kung Shi's feelings.

3. A famous saying states that, "Money can't buy happiness." Why is the Blue Willow legend a good example of what that saying means? Write a paragraph that explains your answer. Be sure to answer the following questions:

   - Which characters have a lot of money? Are they happy?
   - Which characters do not have a lot of money? Are they happy?
   - What is the one thing Kung Shi Fair wants that her father can't buy for her?

37

Story 2

Blue Willow

New Vocabulary
Words

Take out your *Literature Anthology.* Turn to page 16.
What is the title of this story? (Signal.) *"Blue Willow."*
Who is the author? (Signal.) *Pam Conrad.*

1. First we will read some words from the story, and then we will talk about what they mean.
2. Word 1 is **merchant.** What word? (Signal.) *Merchant.*
   - (Repeat for every word in the boxes.)
3. It's your turn to read all the words.
4. Word 1. What word? (Signal.) *Merchant.*
   - (Repeat for every word in the boxes.)

1. merchant	4. embroider	7. turmoil
2. scroll	5. lute	8. topple
3. pavilion	6. reluctance	9. commission
		10. heed

Definitions

(For each definition: First call on a student to read the definition aloud; then present the tasks that go with that definition to the group.)

1. A **merchant** *is a person who buys and sells things.*
   - What are some things a merchant from long ago might sell? (Ideas: *Candles; cloth.*)
2. A **scroll** *is a long piece of fine paper or silk that people write on. A scroll is rolled up when not in use.*
   - What do you call a fine paper or silk that is rolled up when it's not being written on? (Response: *A scroll.*)
3. A **pavilion** *is an open building where you can sit to watch a performance or observe nature.*
   - Where are some places that you might see a pavilion? (Ideas: *At a park; at the beach.*)
4. When you **embroider,** *you sew designs on a cloth.*
   - What are some things that have embroidery on them? (Ideas: *Jeans; shirts; towels.*)
5. A **lute** *is a stringed musical instrument that has an egg-shaped guitar body with the very top part bent back.*
   - In ancient times, lutes were often played to accompany poets as they recited their poems.

16   **Level 6   Literature Guide, Story 2**

6. When you do something with **reluctance,** you do it unwillingly and without enthusiasm.
   - Here's another way of saying **The child did her homework unwillingly and without enthusiasm: The child did her homework with reluctance.**
   - What's another way of saying **The criminal went to jail unwillingly and without enthusiasm**? (Response: *The criminal went to jail with reluctance.*)
7. **Turmoil** *is another way of saying* chaos and confusion.
   - What's another way of saying **After the explosion, the streets were filled with chaos and confusion**? (Response: *After the explosion, the streets were filled with turmoil.*)
8. When things or people **topple,** they fall over.
   - What's another way of saying **The sailors fell over the side of the ship**? (Response: *The sailors toppled over the side of the ship.*)
9. When you **commission** a piece of art, you pay the artist to make the piece of art the way you want it designed.
   - What are you doing when you pay an artist to make something the way you want it to look? (Response: *Commissioning a piece of art.*)
10. When you **heed** what someone tells you, you pay attention and listen to what is said.
    - Here's another way of saying **Make sure you pay attention and listen to my advice: Make sure you heed my advice.**
    - What's another way of saying **Her father didn't pay attention and listen to his daughter's concerns**? (Response: *Her father didn't heed his daughter's concerns.*)

Story Background

1. (Call on individual students to read two or three sentences.)
2. (After students complete a section, ask the questions for that section.)

"Blue Willow" is Pam Conrad's personal interpretation of a Chinese legend. She learned about the legend by way of a Blue Willow plate that was in her family. Blue Willow plates were first made in England during the 1700s, when British culture was greatly influenced by Chinese culture. The pattern on the plates became very popular in England and America. Blue Willow plates are still made and collected today. The legend was inspired by the beautiful pattern. As is typical of legends, there are many versions, but the basic ingredients remain the same.

Pam Conrad wrote her version of the Blue Willow legend when her daughter grew up and fell in love. Pam Conrad's message is one for all parents: Listen to your children and take them seriously when they speak to you about matters of the heart.

- How did the author learn about the Blue Willow legend? (Idea: *From a plate that was in her family.*)
- When and where were Blue Willow plates first made? (Ideas: *In the 1700s in England.*)
- What inspired the legend? (Idea: *The beautiful pattern on the plate.*)
- Why did Pam Conrad write her own version of the legend? (Ideas: *Because her daughter was growing up and had fallen in love; because she wanted to send the message that parents should listen to their children.*)

Much of this legend takes place outdoors. Here are some words particular to this setting that will help you understand and enjoy the story. **Peonies** and **orchids** are flowers known for their beautiful blossoms. **Cassias** and **willows** are types of trees. **Sandpipers** and **cormorants** are birds that are found near water. **Cicadas** are insects that make loud, shrill sounds.

- What are two flowers from the legend that are known for their beautiful blossoms? (Response: *Peonies and orchids.*)
- What are cassias and willows? (Response: *Trees.*)
- What are two birds from the legend that are found near water? (Response: *Sandpipers and cormorants.*)
- What's distinctive about cicadas? (Response: *The sound they make; they make a loud, shrill sound.*)

Water plays an important role in this legend. **Monsoons** are seasonal winds that bring very heavy rains that often result in flooding. **Monsoon rains** can be described as **torrential** because so much water comes down. Other words that describe this intense movement of water are **surging** and **churning.**

- What are monsoons? (Idea: *Seasonal winds that bring torrential rains.*)
- What are some words that describe water that is flowing hard and fast? (Response: *Surging and churning.*)

Jewelry also has a part in this legend. Since Kung Shi Fair is the daughter of a wealthy man, she is used to the finest jewelry made of gold. Gold can be described as **lustrous** because of its luster, or shiny quality. **Trinkets** are cheap jewelry of little or no monetary value. For Kung Shi Fair, trinkets are made of **jade,** a green-colored mineral; of **ivory,** from animal tusks; or of **brass,** an inexpensive metal.

Chang the Good, the young man whom Kung Shi Fair wants to marry, brings her a variety of trinkets as a sign of his affection. To Chang, these are precious treasures, as they had belonged to his mother, who died when he was young. In a simple bundle, he brings necklaces, pendants (necklaces with jewels hanging from them), and bracelets, along with brooches to pin on Kung Shi Fair's clothing.

- What does lustrous mean? (Idea: *shiny.*)
- What's jade? (Idea: *A green-colored mineral.*)
- What's ivory and what's it used for? (Idea: *Animal tusks that are used for jewelry.*)
- What are trinkets? (Idea: *Cheap jewelry.*)
- Why did Chang bring Kung Shi Fair trinkets? (Ideas: *He wanted to show her that he loved her; they were precious to him because they had belonged to his mother.*)
- What's a pendant? (Idea: *A necklace with a jewel hanging from it.*)
- What's a brooch? (Ideas: *A piece of jewelry you wear on your clothes; a piece of jewelry that you pin to your clothes.*)

Story Reading

1. (Call on individual students to read the Focus Questions aloud.)
2. (Remind students to refer to these questions as they read the story to themselves.)

Focus Questions

- Why is Kung Shi Fair's father reluctant to give his daughter the one thing she wants from him?
- Because they love each other, what do Kung Shi Fair and Chang the Good do during the raging storm?
- What lesson does the wealthy merchant learn, and what does he do so others might benefit from his mistakes?

(The story "Blue Willow" is included at this point in the *Literature Guide.*)

Extending Comprehension
Story Questions

1. In what ways does Kung Shi Fair's father spoil her? (Ideas: *He buys her whatever she wants; he builds her a moon pavilion with a stone bridge and found two green frogs to waken her; he buys her a boat he gave her many fine pieces of jewelry.*)

2. Where and how do Chang and Kung Shi Fair meet? (Ideas: *They meet at the river; Kung Shi goes to the shore to look at something that is glistening, and Chang sees her while he is fishing and rows his boat across to her side.*)

3. What is the terrible news delivered by one of the merchant's servants? (Idea: *A leopard is on the rampage.*)

4. What are the different ways the merchant puts off his daughter's most important request? (Ideas: *First he tells her she has to wait until the geese return and the cicadas are quiet, then he says she has to wait until he finds a copper coin, and lastly he tells her she has to wait until there's a rainbow over the stone bridge to her pavilion.*)

5. How does Chang react to the merchant's reluctance? (Ideas: *He's never discouraged; he says something positive; he comes up with a plan.*)

6. What do the villagers decide to do, in spite of the raging storm? (Idea: *Go kill the leopard.*)

7. Why doesn't Chang join the villagers? Where does he go instead? (Ideas: *He doesn't join them because he wants to be with Kung Shi; he goes to her pavilion.*)

8. What does Chang realize when his cormorant brings him something other then a fish from the water? (Ideas: *That Kung Shi is dead; that Kung Shi drowned.*)

9. Where does Kung Shi Fair go during the storm and why? (Ideas: *She goes to her boat to cross the river to tell Chang that his plan with the copper coins didn't work.*)

10. After almost giving up on finding the leopard, the villagers hear a sound. What happens next? (Ideas: *The villagers think the sound is the leopard, so three go off to kill it; they mistakenly kill Chang.*)

11. What do the villagers later figure out about the sound? (Idea: *That it was Chang's heartbroken wail.*)

12. What does the merchant do so his daughter and Chang the Good are never forgotten? (Idea: *He commissions a plate to tell their story.*)

13. What lesson does the merchant learn? (Ideas: *That he should have listened to his daughter because she was asking for what she really wanted; that being rich doesn't guarantee happiness.*)

Discussion Topics

1. Do you think there was a leopard rampaging through the village? How might the legend be different if there hadn't been a leopard? During your discussion, try to answer the following questions:
   - Why do you think a leopard is included as part of the legend?
   - What evidence suggests there was a leopard?
   - What evidence suggests there might not have been a leopard?

2. Water is like a character in this legend. What are some of the important roles that water plays? During your discussion, try to answer the following questions:
   - What different events take place on the river?
   - What happens because of the torrential rains?
   - Could there have been a rainbow over the stone bridge without water?
3. This legend has a tragic ending. How could the deaths of the main characters been avoided? During your discussion, try to answer the following questions:
   - Why didn't Kung Shi Fair know how to use her boat?
   - Why didn't Chang the Good go on the leopard hunt with the other villagers?
   - How are the three villagers feeling as they jump into their boats to go kill the leopard?
   - If Kung Shi Fair's father had agreed to let his daughter marry Chang the Good, would the couple have behaved differently the night of the storm?
4. If you have access to the Internet, go to the following Web site: www.willowcollectors.org/legend.html.
   On the Web site, there is a poem about the Blue Willow legend. Read it aloud. Discuss the similarities and differences between the poem and the story you read.

Writing Ideas

1. Chang is a clever young man. For example, he trains his cormorant to bring fish back to him. Write a letter to Kung Shi Fair's father explaining why Chang is a worthy husband for his daughter.
2. The author uses figurative language, specifically similes, to describe the sound Chang makes when he learns of Kung Shi's death. These examples include: "like the sound of a trapped animal just before it dies" and "like the ragings of a rampaging leopard before it strikes."
   Try to imagine the sound Chang made at that terrible moment and write two of your own similes to describe what you hear. Then try to imagine Kung Shi's fear and horror as the hull of her boat snapped apart and she was pulled into the surging river. Write two more similes to describe Kung Shi's feelings.
3. A famous saying states that, "Money can't buy happiness." Why is the Blue Willow legend a good example of what that saying means? Write a paragraph that explains your answer. Be sure to answer the following questions:
   - Which characters have a lot of money? Are they happy?
   - Which characters do not have a lot of money? Are they happy?
   - What is the one thing Kung Shi Fair wants that her father can't buy for her?

Lesson 60

Materials: Each student will need a copy of the worksheet for lesson 60 (Blackline Master 60).

USING VERB TENSES CONSISTENTLY

1. You've learned that when you write a sentence, you should use verb tenses consistently.

2. That's also true when you write a paragraph. Don't switch back and forth from one tense to another.

3. Look at your worksheet for lesson 60. ✔

• The paragraph describes something that happened in the past, but some of its sentences use present-tense verbs.

• I'll read the paragraph, one sentence at a time. After each sentence, tell me the verb. Then tell me its tense.

• **Gabe stared down from his apartment window.** What's the verb? (Signal.) *Stared.*
  What tense? (Signal.) *Past.*

• **He sees his friends, Rafe and Lucky, on the street below.** What's the verb? (Signal.) *Sees.*
  What tense? (Signal.) *Present.*

• **Rafe wears a top hat.** What's the verb? (Signal.) *Wears.*
  What tense? (Signal.) *Present.*

• **Lucky wore a red cape.** What's the verb? (Signal.) *Wore.*
  What tense? (Signal.) *Past.*

• **Lucky tripped.** What's the verb? (Signal.) *Tripped.*
  What tense? (Signal.) *Past.*

• **He grabs a garbage can.** What's the verb? (Signal.) *Grabs.*
  What tense? (Signal.) *Present.*

4. (Repeat for the rest of the sentences.)

5. Five of the sentences have verbs that express the present tense. What are the numbers of these sentences? (Idea: *Sentences 2, 3, 6, 8, and 10.*)

6. Rewrite these sentences. Change the verbs to past tense. Raise your hand when you've finished.
   (Observe students and give feedback.)

7. (Call on a student to read each rewritten sentence and identify the correct verb tense. If the answer is wrong, give the correct answer.)

Answer Key:

2. He saw his friends, Rafe and Lucky, on the street below.

3. Rafe wore a top hat.

6. He grabbed a garbage can.

8. Rafe and Lucky looked up at Gabe.

10. He bowed deeply to Gabe.

Name _____

Lesson 60

> [1]Gabe stared down from his apartment window. [2]He sees his friends, Rafe and Lucky, on the street below. [3]Rafe wears a top hat. [4]Lucky wore a red cape. [5]Lucky tripped. [6]He grabs a garbage can. [7]Gabe laughed out loud. [8]Rafe and Lucky look up at Gabe. [9]Rafe smiled. [10]He bows deeply to Gabe.

Rewrite only the sentences in the passage that use present-tense verbs. Change the verbs to past tense.

_____

_____

_____

_____

_____

_____

_____

_____

_____

_____

BLM 60 205

ACTIVITY 13

After Lesson 50

Writing: Comparing a Book and a Movie

> **Objective:** Students will determine differences between the novel *Sara Crewe* and a movie based on the book.
>
> **Directions:** Arrange for your class to see the 1995 version of the movie *A Little Princess.* After they have watched the movie, have students read the directions on Blackline Master 8. Have them work in pairs to determine differences between the book and the movie. Then have them tell what they like best about the book and the movie.
>
> **Evaluation:** Students should identify differences between the book and the movie. They should be able to describe differences in characters, setting, and plot. Students should also describe the parts they like best about the book and the movie.

ACTIVITY 13: Comparing a Book and a Movie

Directions: With a partner, make a list of the ways the book and the movie you saw are different. Tell what is different about the characters, setting, and plot. Then list what you liked best in the book and what you liked best in the movie.

	Sara Crewe	*A Little Princess*
Characters		
Setting		
Plot		
What I Liked Best		

Blackline Master 8